THE
RENAISSANCE OF
ITALIAN COOKING

THE
RENAISSANCE OF
ITALIAN COOKING

LORENZA DE 'MEDICI

PHOTOGRAPHS BY JOHN FERRO SIMS

Fawcett Columbine · New York

A Fawcett Columbine Book
Published by Ballantine Books

Text copyright © 1989 by Lorenza de' Medici
Photographs copyright © 1989 by John Ferro Sims

Library of Congress Cataloging-in-Publication Data

Medici, Lorenza de'.
     The renaissance of Italian cooking/Lorenza de' Medici:
photographs by John Ferro Sims. — 1st American ed.
        p.   cm.
     Includes index.
     ISBN 0-449-90364-8
     1. Cookery. Italian.   I. Sims, John Ferro.   II. Title.
TX723.M433   1989
641.5945—dc19   88-47909
                                                     CIP

Manufactured in Italy

First American Edition: October 1989

10   9   8   7   6   5   4   3   2   1

CONTENTS

INTRODUCTION

Several years ago I decided, for a whole convergence of reasons, to give cooking classes. I had already written a series of cookbooks, more like cooking manuals, for an Italian publisher. They were very basic, explaining how to prepare antipasti, how to cook risotto and the like. I adopted the idea from cookbooks I had seen on visits to the United States. At that time – this was in the late nineteen-fifties and early 'sixties – nothing similar existed in Italy and yet the need was growing. During this same period I also initiated a food page for a woman's magazine in which I presented practical menu and recipe suggestions. It was no longer the case that a woman growing up in Italy automatically learned how to cook from her mother or grandmother. The mother was often working and the grandmother was not living with the family. Now, some twenty-five years later, a quite different culinary and cultural development attracted my interest.

Through the years I had viewed life in the Italian kitchen from several if not unique, at least unusual vantage points. While I was growing up, we always had family cooks. The first one I remember well was an Austrian. In those days it was not unusual in Northern Italian families like mine (we lived in Milano) to have foreign cooks. I was about twelve years old then and although I would not want to reconstruct history to the extent of claiming I spent hours at her side while she cooked, my brother and I did pass much of our free time in the family kitchen. Anyhow, I must have picked up a thing or two because something occurred that put my knowledge to the test.

It was during the war and Milano was under occupation. It turned out that our Austrian cook's politics were as Prussian as her pastries and this created a rather sensitive situation for the family. Luckily, a German friend, who was a well-known musician living in Milano, took her off our hands. Her successor was a young woman from the Veneto named Anna. As it was considered a normal part of my education to learn how to run a household by teaching the staff, my mother gave me the task of teaching Anna the family recipes. During that period we had to be inventive in the kitchen as many ingredients were not available. I remember our attempts to camouflage both the taste

Badia a Coltibuono, Chianti

three eldest of our four children were grown, I worked in my own small businesses, first an antique and then a textile store. Compared to Coltibuono, we lived in a relatively small flat in the center of the city and I had to cook and entertain accordingly – with restricted space, time and help.

I think it was this striking juxtaposition of the lifestyles of a Renaissance Tuscan villa and a contemporary city home that brought to the fore the culinary and cultural problem that now interests me. In this sense my life and experience had spanned two completely different eras and I saw that an entire tradition of cooking and entertaining was quickly vanishing because of changing historical and social conditions. How could the precious culinary heritage of the past be adapted so that it would be practical for the twentieth century without losing any of its essential character, either in substance or in style? In recent years I have been attempting to work out an answer to that question at Coltibuono in circumstances very different than those my predecessors enjoyed.

and the texture of the processed cheese which served as a substitute for the real and unavailable item. For some (perhaps patriotic) reason it was called *formaggio Roma* and came in large blocks. Who knows what was inside? Anna and I deep-fried it between two slices of bread, trying to simulate *mozzarella in carrozza*. Meat was simply nonexistent in the city, except on the black market. When some country cousin managed to smuggle us a piece, we found a hundred ways to stretch it. *Crocchette* (meatballs mixed with potatoes, carrots and anything else at hand and then fried) were a favorite. It makes me smile that even in these days when meat is available in superabundance, these same *crocchette*, which I now make as a way of using leftovers, are still a much-in-demand family favorite. All of this turned out to be invaluable experience for me. Anna was a talented and experienced cook who, today, could have worked in any of Milano's best restaurants. As it was, she remained with the family for thirty-five years, until the death of my mother.

Years later, as a young married woman, I found myself in another rather peculiar culinary situation which taught me, among other things, the meaning of that old adage, "too many cooks spoil the broth." In those days, Badia a Coltibuono, the Tuscan wine estate of my husband's family, was administered by my mother-in-law. She was in residence there, however, only during the summer season and brought along her staff, including the cook, from Firenze. We would join her for the month of August. Because she entertained continuously, she would ask me to bring my cook from Milano to help with the extra work. However, fights were always erupting in the kitchen and in order to keep the peace, she had to hire yet a third cook and find something useful for the other two to do in other (and opposite) parts of the house. As heir-apparent to the household, it again fell to me to teach this new cook Coltibuono's culinary traditions.

In almost stark contrast was my normal, everyday life in Milano. My husband is a very active international businessman and, after the

It is also what many friends and acquaintances who have inherited similar situations are endeavoring to do.

A word about this particular tradition of cooking. I think most non-Italians are not aware that historical class structure in Italy had a decisive formative influence on the evolution of Italian cuisine. In other words, Italian cooking has developed its characteristics and variety not only because of regional differences (although a relatively small country, Italy is made-up of twenty-three very distinct regions,) but also because of class differences.

From this perspective Italian cooking can be divided into two general types: what was called the *cucina povera,* an expression that translates as "the cooking of the poor" and connotes simple cooking, and the *cucina alto-borghese* or the cuisine of the upper classes.

The *cucina povera* was the traditional peasant or working-class fare. It was strictly regional, based on local produce – what could be bought at the local market, grown in the garden, fished from the sea or hunted on the land. Because of the lack of any inter-regional transportation system, this type of cuisine was defined by very narrow geographic limits. Even today, in the landlocked part of Chianti where I live, fish cannot be found locally and when a vendor occasionally arrives from the city, he finds customers only among the younger, more venturesome, portion of the population.

Recipes, if they could be called that, were extremely simple. Solid nourishment was the aim of this cooking; yet the food was often prepared with a certain intuitive art for using what was at hand to make it also pleasing and flavorful. (Here Mother Nature has been generous with Italy and a wide variety of herbs was always available even to the poorest of peasants.) These cooking skills were handed down in the kitchen from mother to daughter. Of course, any kind of recipe book would have been totally unheard of. My Coltibuono cook, Romola, who was born on the estate as were her parents, grandparents and great-grandparents before her, is a natural talent in the kitchen and yet she abhors following a written recipe, nor am I able to persuade her to write down any of her many delicious dishes.

The daily menu would have consisted of just one dish: in the South, for example, spaghetti seasoned simply with tomato sauce or olive oil only; in the North, polenta in the Veneto and rice in Lombardia, seasoned with milk or broth. All meals were accompanied by bread. At Coltibuono bread was baked for the tenant farmers every Friday and expected to last the week. On Sundays and feast-days meat with vegetables would have been served. Desserts were made for special occasions only – major holidays such as Christmas and Easter or important family occasions, birthdays, marriages and funerals.

In contrast to this *cucina povera* was the *cucina alto-borghese*. In practice this was the cooking done in the kitchens of the important landed and merchant families of Italy. Although it had regional roots, it was less narrowly local in character. Instead it was diversified, even cosmopolitan, due to the travel possibilities this class of people enjoyed and the cultural intermingling of their families with the frequent foreign occupiers of a region: for example, the Bourbons in Napoli and Sicilia, the French in Piemonte, the Lorraines in Toscana and the Austrians in Lombardia and in the Veneto.

In these kitchens the cooks prepared spaghetti seasoned not just with tomato sauce but enriched with a variety of other ingredients – chicken livers, little meatballs, boiled eggs, béchamel sauce – or even baked in a sweet pastry shell. Polenta was sliced and baked with a cheese sauce and white truffles. Rice was served as a *bomba*, that is, in a mold with a *ragù* of meat and mushrooms. The *cucina alto-borghese* favored local produce but prepared and presented it in a more imaginative and refined way. For this social class eating was not just nourishment but also *un divertimento*.

The traditional *cucina alto-borghese* menu, even a decade or so ago, consisted of six

courses. There would have been an antipasto of cured meats or perhaps a salad with chicken or fish or a vegetable *timballo*; a first course, which for the midday meal consisted of pasta or rice or polenta (depending on the region) and for the evening, a soup; an entremets such as a *frittata* or a vegetable mold; the main course of meat or fish, always accompanied by at least two cooked vegetables and a green, mixed or tomato salad; and to finish off the meal, at midday cheese was usually served and in the evening a dessert, before the final fruit course. It was difficult enough for most adults to get through all of that, let alone children, who were normally served a scaled-down version in their own dining-room. It was not unusual for the family cook or the mistress of the house to commit favorite recipes to paper and these 'cookbooks' were handed down from mother to daughter. When we visited the home of friends, my mother, who was an enthusiastic collector of recipes, had the habit of stealing off to the kitchen in order to give her compliments to the cook and would almost always come away with a few 'secret' family recipes – a trick I have often used to advantage myself.

Carta da musica

This, in brief, is how the classes in Italy ate until well after the Second World War, when the situation began to change, in some cases rapidly, in others more slowly but inevitably. The reasons behind this change were many and they are all interrelated. The upper classes often could no longer afford or in some cases even find the domestic help necessary in order to execute the traditional *cucina alto-borghese*. The peasant or working class now had an income that permitted them to diversify their diet. Many of them left the country for the city, often outside of their native region (e.g. the migration of Southern Italians to the industrial North of Italy) and brought with them their regional culinary traditions. They, in turn, were influenced by the eating habits of the region where they now lived.

Developments in transportation, refrigeration, food packaging, etc., created a wider and more diversified availability of foodstuffs. High-quality fresh produce could be obtained not only in the country but also in the cities. The work schedules of all classes meant a change of eating habits for everyone. Visitors on vacation in Italy and eating mostly in restaurants forget that at home we eat relatively lightly, a first course of rice or pasta (and not always a second course), salad and fruit. Only on Sundays or special holidays do we serve both an antipasto and a dessert.

All of these factors produced significant changes in both these traditional types of Italian cooking. I would say that the remarkable popularity of Italian cuisine during this past decade has been almost exclusively centered around a kind of sophistication of the *cucina povera*, whereas the *cucina alto-borghese* remains virtually unknown. Perhaps this is because it is a family cuisine that historically did not emigrate and as a family cuisine only rarely found its way on to restaurant menus.

My particular interest is the contemporary evolution of the *cucina alto-borghese*. This is the cuisine I serve in my home and that I teach in my classes, which I call "The Villa Table." It is

"Floral" arrangement of cabbages in a Mantuan street

also the food I have been enjoying in recent years in the homes of many of my friends who live in the various regions of Italy. They, too, have adapted their inherited cooking and entertaining traditions according to the necessities of a contemporary lifestyle, without losing any of their unique flavors.

In the course of this book I shall take you on a gastronomic tour, to my home and to the homes, especially the kitchens and dining rooms, of friends who have graciously opened their doors to us and have shared not only favorite menus and recipes but also their hospitality during special occasions – family gatherings, folk *feste*, harvest festivals, cultural and leisure events.

We shall journey to twelve different regions in Italy, each renowned for its gastronomy; visit some splendid homes, and meet many charming and interesting people. Most importantly you will witness a contemporary cultural phenomenon that I like to call the renaissance of Italian cooking, for it embodies all the qualities of Italian civilization that word evokes: classical simplicity, elegance, tradition combined with freshness of approach. I hope you will gain from this tour a unique taste of Italy and bring away not only menus and recipes that are delicious, practical and useful for a variety of home entertainments but also the experience of a particular contemporary Italian way of life rarely enjoyed by visitors.

A NOTE TO THE RECIPES

A person doing home cooking in the kitchen is not in the situation of a chemist experimenting in a laboratory. Not only is it unnecessary, and even impossible, to give exact weights and measurements for some ingredients, and precise instructions for every movement, it can be positively misleading. Far better to leave at least a little room for fantasy. This makes cooking more relaxing and the results better.

For these reasons I steadfastly refuse to be pinned down to exact measurements for certain ingredients, so you will find a fair amount of "a pinch" of this and "a handful" of that in these recipes. A little more or a little less of something rarely makes a decisive difference in a dish and when it does you will be forewarned. Learn to let your sense of smell, touch and taste be your guide and, above all, enjoy cooking.

You may find here and there some cooking terms that are unfamiliar, the references throughout the recipes, for example, to "broth" rather than "stock." I have fully explained the general methods used for making pasta, pastry and broth in the appendix of Basic Italian Cooking Techniques at the end of the recipes on pages 188-189.

All the recipes here are designed for six people, unless otherwise indicated; most of them are easily adaptable to cooking for a smaller or greater number.

PIEMONTE

CASTELLO DI MONALE D'ASTI

*Family reunion in the home of Count Carlo Emanuele Gani and
Countess Nicoletta Balbo Bertone di Sambuy*

First stop on our gastronomic tour is a place where in many ways my own life started out, my grandmother's castle in Piemonte. Here I blissfully passed several weeks of every year until I was eighteen years old. According to my family's very set summer schedule, we spent July and August at the sea and September at my grandmother's. Holidays there were the ones I most looked forward to. During the year at home in Milano there was just my younger brother and myself. At the sea there were lots of other children but we were rather strictly chaperoned. At my grandmother's, however, there were literally a dozen cousins, all about my age, and we had virtually the run of the castle and the little village of Monale beneath it. Of course, my mother always brought a nanny along, but they never seemed much older than ourselves and were more like allies than governesses. One I remember in particular, Fräulein Erna from Austria, was wildly in love with my cousin, Lele, and

*An autumn early morning in Le Langhe and above, the coat of arms
of the Scarampi family on the castle wall*

15

together with his sister, Nicoletta, they would sneak off to the weekly village dances, an area to which our relative freedom did not extend.

Besides the outdoor activities usual in those days – cycling, tennis, walking in the woods and swimming in the river – the absolute highlights of our social calendar were the grape-harvest festival and the annual going-away party given at the castle for the local boys who had been conscripted into the army. These events, especially the latter, held the exciting promise of romance and were often the occasion of "impossible" first love. Other memorable "firsts" of growing up happened here: my first smoke (we used to puff on rolled-up maize leaves), being a bit tipsy for the first time (it was easy to gain access to the wine cellar) as well as some of my first culinary and gastronomic experiences.

Except for special occasions the children always ate in their own dining-room which was located in the cavernous basement of the castle next to the immense kitchen. I remember being most impressed with the family cook,

who wore a proper chef's hat and white jacket. I got the feeling that serious work, even art, was being done down there. We were not, of course, to interfere, but when we brought him the chestnuts we had gathered, he would let us watch him purée them and whip the cream to make a Montebianco just for us. Here I tasted white truffles for the first time, brought as a precious gift to my parents by an uncle from nearby Alba. Best of all, however, were the chilly autumn nights when we would have that most typical Piemontese country dish, *bagna cauda* (literally, "hot bath") – a sauce of olive oil, anchovies, garlic and butter kept warm on the table and into which one dips raw vegetables. My enduring predilection for garlic and raw vegetables most certainly originated with these memorable childhood suppers. In fact, they were so important to all of us that during the war years each of our families would pool the scanty portions of olive oil they had been able to set aside in order that we might continue to enjoy this traditional feast.

The castle of Monale has been in my family

for just over six hundred years. It was bought in 1387 by the Scarampi family. My grand-mother, Paola Scarampi and her sister, Adele, were the only children of the last male Scarampi. In 1884, Adele married Count Carlo Gani, the grandfather of my cousin, Carlo Emanuele, and in 1885, Paola Scarampi married my grandfather, Marquess Edoardo de' Medici dei Principi d'Ottaiano.

The original Scarampi were, I must confess, those infamous moneylenders of the Middle Ages. It seems they wheeled and dealed all over Europe, especially in the prosperous capitals of the North, where, it would appear from a fourteenth-century Flemish statue, the worst name you could call an enemy or even a friend in the heat of argument was, "you ——— Scarampi!" Such foul language carried a heavy fine. By Renaissance times, however, they had become respectable (and rich) bankers but family fortunes suffered a setback during Napoleon's time. They made the mistake of backing him against Piemonte's Casa di Savoia, which became the royal family of a newly united Italy. The Savoia, one of my cousins was fond of saying, were still tending sheep while his family had already built their kingdom.

It is again in September that I am returning to my grandmother's castle, but this time with my husband, Piero, and our daughter, Ema-nuela, for the wedding of Alessandra, the daughter of my cousin, Carlo Emanuele Gani and his wife, Ada. Carlo Emanuele and his sister, Nicoletta Balbo Bertone di Sambuy, are the present owners and inhabitants of the castle. It is also going to be the occasion for a grand family reunion. About twenty relatives have been invited to spend the weekend. The marriage ceremony and celebration will be held on Saturday late afternoon. Friday evening there is to be a supper for all the cousins and on Sunday afternoon, a farewell luncheon to the bride and groom for family and very close friends.

From a purely gastronomic point of view, late September is a perfect time to visit

A typical Piemontese landscape of maize and vines

The courtyard of the castle

Piemonte. I always think of its cuisine as autumnal in character, because so many of its basic ingredients come to maturity during this season: truffles, with which the fortunate Piemontesi are able to flavor almost every dish – on eggs "sunny side up" seems to me the height of gourmandise abandon; cardoons, an edible white thistle that is the distinguishing mark of authentic *bagna cauda piemontese*; grapes and walnuts that compliment many a dessert as well as other dishes of this region; partridge, pheasant and the several other kinds of small game that form the substance of grand repasts both in homes and in restaurants.

As one drives from Milano to Monale, the landscape changes quite abruptly from the flat and monotonous Lombard plain to the rather precipitous terrain of Piemonte, which means "foot of the mountains," in this case, the Alps. Monale is located not far from Alba, truffle capital of Italy, in the township of Asti, renowned for its sparkling wine, *spumante* (literally, "foaming") – just one of many French influences on the way people eat and drink in this region. The local wine is Barbera and a veritable sea of vineyards stretches as far as the eye can see. At this season large bunches of big, dark red grapes hang heavy on the vine. Monale no longer produces its own wine as it did when I was growing up, but my cousin, Dado Dal Pozzo, who owns nearby Castello di Canale, makes many fine wines and he is sure to bring a generous supply for tonight's reunion.

In many ways Monale is a picture-book castle, perched on top of one of the precipitous little hills that dot this pre-Alpine area much like the whipped-cream swirls that top a Montebianco, the delicious dessert specialty of

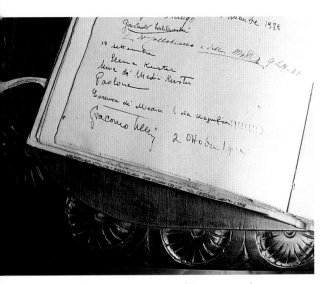

As a young girl Lorenza signs the visitor's book "la Magnifica"

the region. Notwithstanding a bit of urban sprawl with the concrete and steel buildings it implies, the village of Monale still manages to run picturesquely down the hill, much as I remember it from my childhood. As it now appears, the exterior of the castle dates from the eighteenth century, when the medieval harshness of the original edifice was softened and made more harmonious by the local red brick so typical of this part of Piemonte. Its massive walls and two standing towers, however, rise out of the original foundations, built in the early twelfth century as a fortification by the first feudal lords of the area.

Winding up the hill – past the church where the marriage ceremony will take place and the cemetery where my mother and father are buried – one arrives at the baroque entrance gates to the castle. These open on to an immense and gracious eighteenth-century courtyard, sections of which, the upper loggia, for example, were restored during the last century in neo-Gothic style. The castle forms a U shape around the courtyard. During my childhood one wing of the building belonged to my family and the other to my aunt and uncle, Enrichetta and Raimondo Gani and their

family. Now it is divided between the families of their two children, Carlo Emanuele and Nicoletta.

It is Carlo Emanuele, called Lele, who greets us at the gates, accompanied by his three beloved rough-haired dachshunds. For many years Lele managed large fruit plantations in the Belgian Congo and he now lives in semiretirement at Monale, where he relishes his life as country squire and scholar, putting the family archives in order and attending to the unending task of restoring the castle. This evening he and his wife, Ada, are hosting the cousins in their apartments. Although death has somewhat diminished our number, with spouses included we form a perfect complement of twenty, all comfortably settled into the numerous bedroom suites of the castle.

Tonight supper is served in the intimacy of the library. Its walls are lined with volumes that reflect the interests of the family over the centuries – navigation, exploration, art history and nineteenth-century English literature. A large fire warms the chilly autumn evening and in the center of the room is set an enormous round table I remember from my childhood. Lele's father, whose hobby was woodworking, had crafted it years ago just for the children. Built into its center is a kind of a huge lazy Susan and it easily sits all twenty of us. Ada has prepared a surprise for their "Chianti cousin," my favorite Piemontese specialty, *bagna cauda*. It is the perfect choice for this evening's family reunion, because it is a dish that transforms a meal into a restorative communal event. We all gather round and dip the assortment of sliced raw vegetables into the aromatic sauce that is kept hot in an earthenware chafing dish placed on the lazy Susan. Supper is washed down with large draughts of Dado's lively red wine and the hours pass in sweet and savory reminiscences. As the evening comes to an end, my cousin, Nicoletta, draws my attention to the ancient guest book laying on the library table and to an entry made in September 1937, where with my usual modesty, she comments,

I had signed myself, "Lorenza la Magnifica." Ah well, the folly of youth!

Early the next morning preparations are well underway for the wedding feast. Over one hundred guests have been invited for a sit-down buffet supper. All the reception rooms of the castle have been opened and filled with flowers for the celebration and numerous tables are being set in the courtyard, where the rose beds surrounding the ancient well have stayed in late bloom especially for the occasion. The baroque village church just outside the castle walls is festooned with garlands of grapes and wild flowers for the late-afternoon nuptial Mass. Today my particular responsibility is organizing the production of several hundred chestnut truffles and luckily for me the women have already husked the heaps of chestnuts we will need.

After the marriage ceremony the guests, who include all the village dignitaries, return to the castle for the wedding banquet. Waiters in white jackets are already passing with trays of several kinds of finger food and filling glasses with fine dry spumante from Asti. For the first course there are colorful platters of peppers stuffed with rice, tomatoes in green sauce and grape salad, followed by two Piemontese cold meat dishes, *vitello tonnato* (veal with tuna sauce) and *polpettone di Monale* (meat loaf stuffed with pistachios and ham.) Judging by all

Nineteenth-century family silverware

the empty dessert plates surrounding me, my idea of adding an orange flavor to the traditional wedding cake was obviously a success.

As night descends, dancing begins on the castle lawns. The music is a blend of traditional waltzes and polkas and contemporary disco and the townsfolk are invited to join in. Torches are lit, accentuating the medieval aspect of the castle and illuminating the ancient scroll under the sixteenth-century sundial that dominates the southern wall of the courtyard. It strikes me that the inscription is an appropriate *augurio* or good-luck wish on the occasion of both the wedding and the family reunion: *Nulla fluat cuius no meminisse velis,* whose sentiment, freely translated, could be: "May all your memories be happy ones."

Alessandra and her husband, Elio, spend their wedding night in the castle in order to be present at a farewell luncheon on Sunday with family and the close friends who have traveled from afar to attend their marriage celebration. My cousin, Nicoletta, is hostess at this meal, which is served in the large formal dining room of the castle. Imaginative as ever, Nicoletta has printed the menu on individual cards that are reproductions of one hand-painted almost one hundred years ago for my grandmother by the artist, Davide Calandra. The dishes are simple, elegant and classically Piemontese: a tasty dish of polenta served with braised beef in a Barolo wine sauce, glazed carrots and onions, and baked apples with a cream sauce and amaretti cookies.

Maybe more than any other of the forty-some rooms of the castle, this dining-room is the one most filled with memories for me. As was the custom, the walls and ceiling were redecorated on the occasion of my grand-parents' wedding and their combined coat of arms, the Scarampi and the de'Medici, are prominently featured. The room is furnished with family heirlooms – seventeeth-century Piemontese tables, chairs, sideboards, ancient Northern Italian pewter jugs and drinking

The ornate papered ceiling of the drawing room

mugs and a collection of Sèvres porcelain. Several large family portraits preside over the scene. Sitting here after dinner, surrounded by family past and present and feeling quite mellow as I sip a glass of my cousin Dado's excellent Grappa, I am startled out of my reverie by something I never remarked upon before. In her portrait my grandmother, Paola de'Medici, is wearing above her wedding band an emerald surrounded by tiny diamonds. It is the very same ring that I am wearing now and that my mother wore and gave to me at the time of my engagement. What a nice surprise to have noticed this after all these years and what a fitting way to end the celebration of a family wedding and reunion.

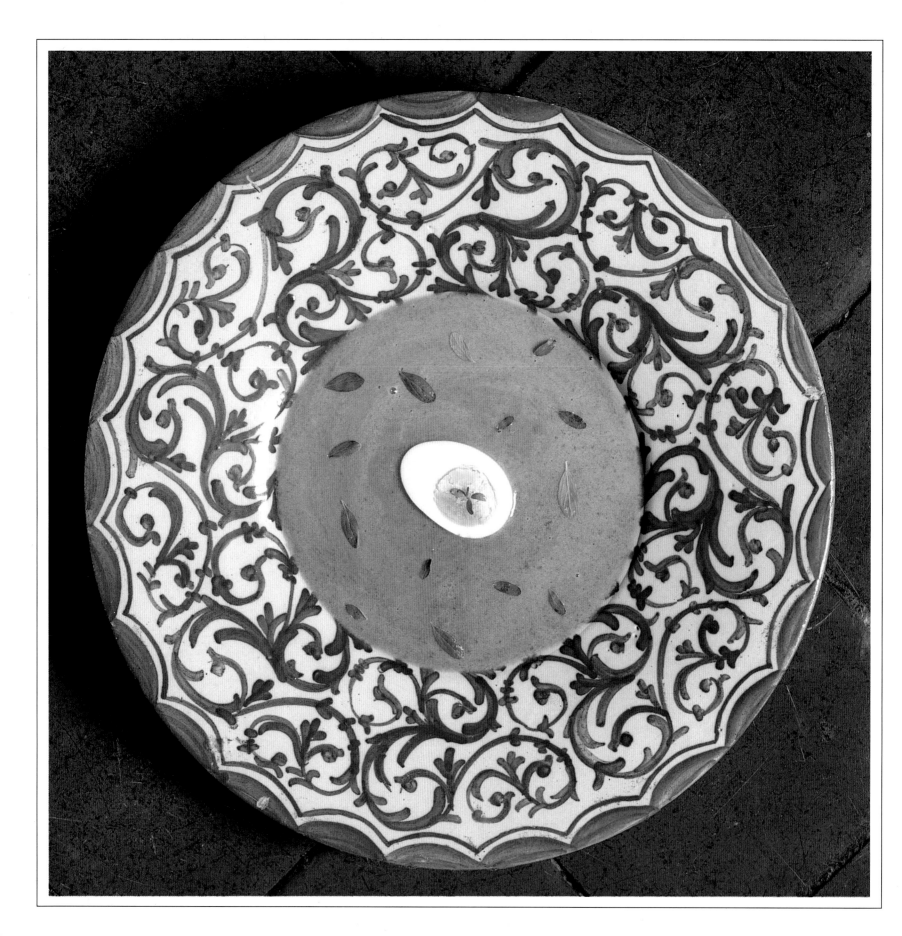

MENU FOR A FAMILY REUNION

CREMA DI POMODORO
Eggs with tomato cream

CARDO IN BAGNA CAUDA
Cardoon in hot anchovy dip

BUDINO DI AMARETTI
Amaretti mold

In Piemonte, cardoons are the traditional vegetable for *bagna cauda*, but many others are suitable: sliced bell peppers, broccoli stalks, celery, artichokes, crisp spinach leaves, etc. For a more substantial meal, after the vegetables are done break an egg for every participant into the pot and fry or scramble them in the rest of the sauce.

Suggested Wines   All the garlic will bring on a thirst for lots of young robust Barbera from Alba or Asti.

CREMA DI POMODORO
Eggs with tomato cream

1 onion
1 carrot
1 celery stalk
2 oz/4 tbsp/50 g butter
2 lb/1 kg fresh, ripe tomatoes
1 tbsp sugar
salt and pepper
1 handful fresh marjoram leaves
16 fl oz/2 cups/450 ml milk
3 hard-boiled eggs

Chop the onion, carrot, celery and cook in the butter over low heat for about 10 minutes.

Slice the tomatoes into small pieces and add to the pan with the sugar, salt, pepper and half the marjoram. Cook for 15 minutes. Add the milk, then purée the mixture through a food mill or food processor.

Cut the hard-boiled eggs in half lengthwise and place on 6 plates, yolks up. Reheat the tomato mixture, pour around the eggs, sprinkle with the rest of the marjoram and serve.

CARDO IN BAGNA CAUDA
Cardoon in hot anchovy dip

1 large cardoon
juice of 1 lemon
6 garlic cloves, chopped
2 oz/4 tbsp/50 g butter
8 fl oz/1 cup/225 ml extra virgin olive oil
6 anchovy fillets in oil
salt

Clean the cardoon by removing the harder outer stalks and strings. Slice thinly, then cut into pieces 3 in/7.5 cm long. Blanch for 1 minute, cool under cold running water and transfer to a serving bowl with the lemon and water to cover. Place the bowl and chafing dish in the center of the table.

In a small saucepan, heat the butter and oil, add the anchovies with oil and cook over low heat until they begin to disintegrate. Season with salt, add the chopped garlic, and pour

into the chafing dish and bring to a simmer.

Your guests should be invited to take a piece of cardoon and dip it into the sauce, letting it cook for a minute before eating.

BUDINO DI AMARETTI
Amaretti mold

6 egg yolks
8 oz/1 cup/225 g sugar
3 tbsp powdered (unflavored) gelatine
16 fl oz/2 cups/450 ml milk
7 oz/generous 1 cup/200 g bittersweet chocolate bits
22 amaretti biscuits (cookies)

Put the egg yolks and sugar in a bowl and beat together with a wire whisk until they thicken.

Dissolve the gelatine in the milk and melt the chocolate in a double boiler over low heat.

Add the melted chocolate and the milk to the egg yolk mixture, then return to the double boiler and cook until the cream thickens. Whisk continuously, without letting it boil.

Pulverize 16 of the amaretti in a food processor and stir into the cream. Pour the mixture into a ring mold and chill for at least four hours.

Unmold onto a serving dish, garnish with the remaining whole amaretti and serve.

Crema di pomodoro

Budino di amaretti
Cardo in bagna cauda

homemade. Serve the chestnut truffles with after-dinner coffee.

Suggested Wines The region of Piemonte has so many fine wines to choose from. You may want to do as we did for Alessandra's wedding: a brut spumante as an aperitif, my cousin Dado's dry, white Arneis from the vineyards of Malabaila di Canale with the vegetable dishes, a great Barbaresco with the meat, and the absolutely delicious Moscato d'Asti Spumante with dessert and after.

CARNE CRUDA AL LIMONE
Raw meat on lemon slices

7 oz/1 cup/200 g minced (ground) lean beef
salt and pepper
grated peel of 1 lemon
juice of ½ lemon
3 tbsp extra virgin olive oil
6 lemon slices
6 radishes

In a bowl mix the meat with the salt, pepper, lemon peel, lemon juice and olive oil. Arrange the slices of lemon on a serving dish. On each put a tablespoon of meat mixture, and top with a radish cut like a flower.

PEPERONI RIPIENI DI RISO
Peppers stuffed with rice

6 red bell peppers
12 tbsp Arborio rice
salt and pepper
2 cloves garlic
3 anchovy fillets in oil
2 oz/4 tbsp/50 g butter
2 tbsp chopped parsley
1 tbsp extra virgin olive oil

Cook the peppers in the oven at 375°F/190°C/Mark 5 for about 20 minutes.

Cut off the tops and scrape out the seeds. Cook the rice in a pan of salted boiling water for about 15 minutes. Drain.

Chop the garlic and mash the anchovy fillets. Cook in a frying pan in the butter over a low heat. Add the rice, stir for a couple of seconds and add the parsley. Stuff the peppers with this mixture. Arrange in an oiled baking dish and return to the oven for 5 minutes before serving.

POMODORI IN SALSA VERDE
Tomatoes with green sauce

6 ripe tomatoes
2 anchovy fillets in oil
1 tbsp capers
2 tbsp soft fresh breadcrumbs
3 fl oz/⅓ cup/75 ml red wine vinegar
1 hard-boiled egg
3 tbsp chopped parsley
4 fl oz/½ cup/125 ml extra virgin olive oil
salt and pepper

Cut off the tops of the tomatoes, scrape out the seeds only, and arrange on a platter.

Mash the anchovy fillets, chop the capers, soak the breadcrumbs in the vinegar and squeeze dry. Chop the egg.

Put all these ingredients into a bowl, add the parsley, olive oil and salt and pepper and mix well. Fill the tomatoes with the sauce before serving.

INSALATA DI UVA
Grape salad

1 lb/450 g green table grapes
10 oz/300 g fontina cheese
1 apple
½ bottle dry white wine
salt and pepper
1 tsp lemon juice
4 tbsp extra virgin olive oil

MENU FOR A WEDDING RECEPTION

CARNE CRUDA AL LIMONE
Raw meat on lemon slices

PEPERONI RIPIENI DI RISO
Peppers stuffed with rice

POMODORI IN SALSA VERDE
Tomatoes with green sauce

INSALATA DI UVA
Grape salad

VITELLO TONNATO
Cold veal with tuna sauce

POLPETTONE DI MONALE
Monale meatloaf

TORTA DELLA SPOSA
Wedding cake

TARTUFI DI CASTAGNE
Chestnut truffles

For practical purposes I have given ingredients for the usual six persons, but the recipes are all suitable for larger numbers and the amounts can be multiplied accordingly. The lemon slices with raw meat should be served as an appetizer with the aperitif. The meat can either be minced (ground) or very thinly sliced. The other dishes (with the exception of the sweets, of course) can be placed on the buffet table together. They all combine well.

A word about polpettone. Meatloaf sounds mundane in English (and perhaps tastes that way) but not so polpettone in Italy. We season it highly and boiling keeps it light in texture as well as taste. It also provides a delicious broth.

As wedding cakes go, this is certainly uncomplicated and one that can really be

Carne cruda al limone

1 handful shelled walnuts, roughly chopped
2-3 handfuls mixed green salad leaves

Cut the cheese into julienne strips and reserve.

Put the grapes in a bowl. Peel and dice the apple and add to the bowl of grapes. Pour in the wine and let the fruit marinate for a couple of hours.

Drain the fruit and arrange on a salad plate with the cheese. Add salt, pepper, lemon juice, and olive oil and mix well. Sprinkle over the nuts surround with the salad leaves and serve.

VITELLO TONNATO
Cold veal with tuna sauce

For the veal:
60 fl oz/7½ cups/1.7 liters water
18 oz/500 g eye round (or top round) veal
1 celery stalk
1 carrot
1 bunch parsley
1 bay leaf
salt

For the sauce:
2 egg yolks
1 egg
pinch of salt
8 fl oz/1 cup/225 ml extra virgin olive oil
8 oz/1¼ cups/250 g tuna
3 anchovy fillets in oil
2 tbsp capers
juice of 2 lemons
4 fl oz/½ cup/125 ml milk

For the veal, bring the water to the boil. Add the meat and remaining ingredients, then simmer for 2 hours over low heat. Drain the meat, cool and slice thinly. Arrange the slices overlapping on a platter.

To make the sauce, combine egg yolks, egg, and pinch of salt in a blender. Add the oil in a thin stream. When a mayonnaise forms, add the tuna, anchovies, capers, lemon juice and milk. Blend to a creamy consistency. Pour the sauce over the meat and serve.

POLPETTONE DI MONALE
Monale meatloaf

1 handful soft fresh breadcrumbs
8 fl oz/1 cup/225 ml milk
3½ oz/½ cup/100 g chopped ham
3½ oz/½ cup/100 g chopped mortadella
8 oz/1 cup/225 g minced (ground) beef
8 oz/1 cup/225 g minced (ground) lean veal
3½ oz/¾ cup/100 g grated Parmesan cheese
1 egg
1 handful pistachio nuts
1 tbsp chopped parsley

salt and pepper
2 tbsp plain (all-purpose) flour
2 oz/4 tbsp/50 g butter
1 tbsp extra virgin olive oil
1 carrot
1 onion
1 celery stalk
1 bunch parsley
1 clove
1 bay leaf

Soak the breadcrumbs in the milk and squeeze dry. Put the ham and mortadella in a mixing bowl together with the ground beef and veal, Parmesan, egg, pistachios, breadcrumbs, chopped parsley and salt and pepper. Mix well and knead for about 5 minutes. Form the meat mixture into a loaf at least 2 in/5 cm in diameter and sprinkle with flour.

In a frying pan heat the butter and oil. Put in the meatloaf and brown over moderate heat on all sides, turning gently, until a crust is formed. Wrap the meatloaf in a cloth, tie well and put in a casserole of salted, boiling water with the carrot, onion, celery, parsley, clove and bay leaf. Cover and cook over low heat for about 1 hour.

When cooked, remove from broth, unwrap, place on a platter and cover with another dish. Allow to cool completely. To serve, slice and arrange on a platter.

TORTA DELLA SPOSA
Wedding cake

7 oz/1 cup less 2 tbsp/200 g sugar
1 tbsp water
pinch of salt
6 eggs, separated
grated peel of ½ lemon
6 tbsp plain (all-purpose) flour
1 tbsp potato flour (or cornstarch)
1 oz/2 tbsp/25 g butter
12 sugar cubes
1 orange
2 tbsp sweet white wine

1 tbsp brandy
8 fl oz/1 cup/225 ml whipping cream
8 oz/2 cups/225 g shelled walnuts

Mix the sugar with the water, salt, egg yolks, lemon peel, sifted flour and potato flour. Beat the egg whites to firm peaks and fold in.

Butter 2 spring-clip (springform) pans of different dimensions, 6 in/15 cm and 7 in/18 cm, and pour in the mixture. Bake in the oven at 350°F/180°C/Mark 4 for 40 minutes. Allow to cool then remove from pans.

Peel the orange rind (not the pith) into wide strips and rub the sugar cubes on the cut surface until well coated. Put into a bowl, squeeze the orange juice on top, add wine and brandy. Mix until sugar has dissolved. Beat the cream to stiff peaks and chop half the nuts.

Spread the larger of the cakes with half of the wine mixture, cover with a layer of cream, and sprinkle over the chopped nuts. Place the smaller cake on top, pour over the rest of the wine mixture, and decorate with the cream using a piping (pastry) bag. Decorate with the remaining walnuts and refrigerate until ready to serve.

TARTUFI DI CASTAGNE
Chestnut truffles

2¼ lb/1 kg chestnuts
4 oz/½ cup/125 g sugar
4 fl oz/½ cup/125 ml milk
10 oz/1⅔ cups/300 g bittersweet chocolate bits
2 oz/½ cup/50 g cocoa powder

Put the chestnuts in a pan, cover with cold water and simmer for about 20 minutes. Remove the shell, peel off the inner skin and purée through a food mill or processor. Add the sugar and milk, mix and cook for a couple of minutes. Melt the chocolate over low heat and add the purée. Mix well and let cool.

Form the mixture into nut-size balls and chill. When cold, roll them in the cocoa powder, arrange on a platter and serve.

Pomodori in salsa verde

MENU FOR A SUNDAY LUNCHEON

POLENTA CON BRASATO
Polenta with braised beef

CAROTE E CIPOLLE GLASSATE
Glazed carrots and onions

MELE ALLA CREMA
Baked apples with a cream sauce

I have a predilection for *piatto unico* meals, where only one plate is served and no hectic last-minute preparations are necessary. Braised meats are a Northern Italian favorite. We use the poorer cuts of meat that have good flavor, marinate and cook them for hours so they become tender. It is essential to brown the meat well and not to add all the wine marinade at once or else the flavor will boil away.

Suggested Wines   A meal at which to savor with friends that prized bottle of Barolo, *riserva speciale*, hidden in the cellar.

POLENTA CON BRASATO
Polenta with braised beef

For the braised beef:
2 oz/50 g pancetta
2¼ lb/1 kg beef, suitable for braising
1 bottle aged Barolo wine
1 carrot
1 onion
2 celery stalks
1 bay leaf
1 tbsp peppercorns
1 clove
½ oz/10 g dried porcini mushrooms
2 tbsp plain (all-purpose) flour
2 oz/4 tbsp/50 g butter

salt
For the polenta:
60 fl oz/7½ cups/1.5 liters water
1 tbsp sea salt
13 oz/2⅔ cups/375 g coarse maize flour (yellow cornmeal)
3½ oz/7 tbsp/100 g butter

To make the braised beef, slice the pancetta, slit the meat in several places, insert the slices, put in a bowl and pour over the red wine. Cut the carrot into julienne strips, slice the onion and the celery and add to the meat together with the bay leaf, pepper and clove. Marinate for 8 hours, turning from time to time.

Soak the dried mushrooms in cold water for 1 hour, squeeze them dry with your fingers, strain off and reserve the soaking liquid. Drain the marinade from the meat, and reserve. Dry the meat well with paper towels and dust with flour.

Heat the butter in a flameproof casserole and brown the meat on all sides over high heat. When golden brown, pour half the marinade into the casserole with all the seasoning and vegetables. Turn the heat to low, add salt and mushrooms, cover and cook for 3 hours, adding the rest of the marinade a little at a time.

About an hour before the meat is done, make the polenta. Boil the water with the salt and pour in the maize flour, mixing with a whisk. Cook for about 40 minutes, stirring from time to time with a wooden spoon.

Remove from heat, add the butter, mix well and pour the polenta into a wet bowl. Press down and smooth the surface. Transfer it to a wooden cutting board and cover with a cloth to keep hot until time to serve.

Put the meat on a serving platter and keep warm. Purée the remaining contents of the casserole with a food processor. Return to the casserole with the reserved mushroom liquid. Cook until the sauce takes on the consistency of cream. Slice the meat, pour over the sauce and serve with the polenta.

CAROTE E CIPOLLE GLASSATE
Glazed carrots and onions

1 lb/450 g baby onions
1 lb/450 g carrots
salt and pepper
1 tbsp butter
1 tbsp extra virgin olive oil
6 tbsp sugar
3 fl oz/⅓ cup/75 ml red wine vinegar

Blanch onions for about 10 minutes. Drain and peel. Cut carrots into bite-size pieces and blanch. Put the onions and carrots in a saucepan with the butter and oil and simmer for 30 minutes, adding 1 glass of water.

Dissolve sugar in vinegar and boil for 5 minutes. Pour over onions and carrots. Allow sauce to reduce to desired consistency and serve.

MELE ALLA CREMA
Baked apples with cream sauce

6 tbsp raisins
3½ fl oz/7 tbsp/100 ml dessert wine
1 oz/2 tbsp/25 g sugar
8 fl oz/1 cup/225 ml whipping cream
2 tbsp Grand Marnier
6 Golden Delicious apples
1 tbsp butter, for greasing the pan
6 amaretti biscuits (cookies)

Soak raisins in the dessert wine for about 1 hour. Dissolve the sugar in a saucepan over

Polenta

moderate heat, stirring occasionally. At the same time, heat half the cream. When the sugar has caramelized add the cream to the sugar, mixing well together. Add the Grand Marnier and leave to cool.

Whip the rest of the cream until firm and add to the cooled sauce, leaving some aside for decorating at the end.

Peel and core the apples and fill with the raisins. Arrange in a greased pan, add a little water and bake in the oven at 350°F/180°C/ Mark 4 for about 30 minutes. Allow to cool, then pour over the sauce. Decorate with the remaining cream and crumble over the amaretti biscuits.

LIGURIA

CAPO SANTA CHIARA A GENOVA

Recipes from the Riviera at the home of Giovanna Cameli

If I were to follow a geographical itinerary on this culinary tour, we would enter Liguria over the Maritime Alps that divide it from Piemonte. My usual route, however, is from my home in Toscana, which borders this region on the southeast, and my favorite season to make the trip is Easter. At this time of year you feel the weather ought to be pleasantly mild and the countryside in bright flower. Yet in the Chianti hills where I live it can often be quite gloomy and rainy, the countryside still

bleak and barren. Tradition dictates that our potted lemon trees should come out of their winter quarters and into the garden for Easter but there is always the fear, especially if the feast comes early in the season, that they will be nipped by frost or even sprinkled with snow.

By this time in Liguria, however, there can be no doubt that spring has fully arrived. As you drive along the coast, in and out of the seemingly endless succession of tunnels

Decorated houses along the seafront, Santa Margherita Ligure, and above,
interior of the house of Giovanna Cameli at Capo Santa Chiara

31

through the Apennines, which at this point advance straight to the sea, you catch glimpses of bougainvillaea cascading down the cliffs to the deep blue water below. We are traveling along the Riviera di Levante, the eastern stretch of Liguria's two hundred miles of coast, a narrow crest of shore and mountains with the bay of Genova and its port more or less at its center and on its western side the Riviera di Ponente stretching to the French border. Coming from the direction of Toscana one passes through all the fabulous towns of the Italian Riviera – Portovenere, where Lord Byron is buried, Rapallo, Santa Margherita Ligure, Portofino and Camogli.

From high terraced farms with carefully tended parcels of land wafts the fragrance of Liguria, always the first characteristic of this region to welcome me when I arrive. It is also a foretaste of the aromatic cooking to come. Even as early as late March the azure star blossoms of borage are blooming along road-banks and in fields. In Genova this edible herb with a decided flavor of cucumber is used as a stuffing for ravioli, just as the Tuscans use spinach. It is also their traditional filling for a *frittata*, an Italian omelet, and a seasoning in many regional dishes. Its young leaves and flowers are lovely in salad as well.

Maggiorana, sweet marjoram, is another fragrant herb that scents the gentle air and local cooking, particularly its soups and fish dishes and in the classical nut sauce that goes over *pansoti*, triangular ravioli. The filling for these *pansoti* as well as a seasoning for rice and soup is *preboggion*, a little bouquet of edible weeds gathered from the fields that includes, according to the season, such plants as dandelion, pimpernel, thistle, wild chervil and radicchio.

Of course, the king of Ligurian herbs, whose name is derived from the Greek word meaning royal, and the most fragrant of them all, is *basilico*. Basil grows in great bunches in country

gardens and in little pots on windowsills in the city. It is the essence, in the fullest sense of the word, of that most characteristic sauce of Ligurian cuisine, *pesto*.

As one might imagine about something so intimately connected with a region's culinary identity as pesto, there are various versions of the classical recipe. The basic ingredients and fundamental techniques, however, are fixed. As its name from the Italian word to pound or crush implies, pesto is made by crushing with a mortar and pestle a bunch of fresh basil leaves, a clove or two of garlic, a pinch of salt, a handful of pine nuts and a bit of pecorino cheese. When these have been ground into a fine paste, some olive oil is mixed in until it becomes a smooth sauce, fresh green in color. This much, at least, is canonical. Butter is not added in the old recipes, neither are walnuts or Parmesan cheese mentioned.

There are several refinements and adaptations of the process. Naturally the Genoese hold that authentic pesto can only be made with their particularly aromatic short-leafed variety of basil, picked before the flowers come into bud. A marble mortar (Carrara is just down the coast in Toscana) and a pestle of quality hard wood should be used, because they are ideal for releasing the full flavor of the ingredients and grinding them to a perfect consistency. Of course, one can make a very satisfactory pesto with the more common large-leaf variety of basil, Parmesan cheese and even using a food processor.

Now here is a helpful hint for making pesto that I recently picked up at the home of my Genoese friend, Giovanna Cameli, when I remarked on the tender green color of her pesto. Usually when pesto comes into contact with hot food it discolors. Maria, her cook for twenty-five years, told me the only way to retain its fresh color is to use the leaves of plants that are no more than three inches high. She keeps little trays of these in the garden,

Exterior of the house

pulls up the whole plant when its leaves are ready and reseeds continuously in order to maintain her supply.

Giovanna lives in a lovely seventeenth-century house at the tip of Capo Santa Chiara in Genova's Boccadasse district, a promontory jutting into the sea that until the last century was a fishing village inhabited largely by underwater divers who worked in Genova's ship-building industry. Although it is just a few minutes' drive from the bustling port of the city, the largest in Italy, from her terraced garden on steep cliffs overlooking the sea, she enjoys an unobstructed view of the Ligurian coast as far as Portofino where she also has a summer villa. Giovanna is a woman of great style and creative energy, who designs and manufactures elegant household articles in Perspex. She sells to the best shops in Italy and her beautiful creations decorate the finest homes from Milano to Roma.

Giovanna has invited me to spend the Easter holidays. Religious feasts seem to have particular importance in Liguria, perhaps because of its connection with the sea. At any rate, Giovanna has an unusual and congenial custom for Easter Sunday. At noon the parish priest comes to celebrate Mass in her home for family and friends. This is the occasion for a festive luncheon afterward which she serves on her splendid terrace with its spectacular view.

By long-established tradition, the first course is one of the epicurian masterpieces of Genoese gastronomy, the *torta pasqualina*, Easter pie. All Giovanna's guests look forward to this dish with great expectations because Maria still makes it according to the original recipe with twenty-four layers of transparently thin pastry.

The *torta pasqualina* is basically a vegetable tart that has been refined to perfection over the centuries. It is made with the small variety of artichokes with long, narrow, violet-colored leaves. They are at their best during this season and Maria uses only the most tender leaves and hearts. After these have been seasoned with

Dining room display of pottery and silverware

garlic, borage and marjoram and cooked with olive oil, they are blended with a rich sauce of fresh ricotta, Parmesan cheese and egg. She spoons this mixture between the twenty-four layers of pastry, twelve on the bottom and twelve on top. Before adding the top sheets, she makes twelve little wells in the filling and pours a whole raw egg into each one. As the pie bakes these become hard and when it is sliced their golden yolks add a richness of color as well as taste to the dish. Under Maria's experienced hand the dough has puffed up into twenty-four (countable) flaky, golden layers. I hope I have not gone against any religious symbolism by reducing in my recipe the number of layers of dough and eggs to six. After all, this is a Paschal pie and there were twelve guests at the original Paschal supper. Even at six it is a most worthy dish for a festive occasion and if you are in Liguria you can buy a quite decent rendition in this region's excellent food shops.

For the second course of her luncheon, Giovanna serves what is perhaps the most celebrated Genoese fish dish, *cappon magro*. This is an extraordinarily elaborate combination and construction of ingredients with an ancient,

more humble past. In fact, as a datum in the history of gastronomy, it is one of the most interesting examples of the heights (also literally, in this case) that an originally "poor man's" dish has reached through centuries of imaginative development. It grew out of the simple ingredients, a little fresh fish and a few fresh vegetables, that a sailor was able to pick up in port and put on his piece of ship's biscuit, the hard, coarse bread kept on board, that he rubbed with garlic and doused with olive oil. (*Cappon* is the name for that garlicky, oiled bread and has no relation to a castrated cock!)

As it is served now, *cappon magro* is a lavish fish and vegetable salad with a green sauce, abounding with the sights, scents and savor of the Mediterranean. It still begins from its humble roots of a ship's biscuit rubbed with garlic and soaked in sea water. Upon this, alternate layers of various fish and vegetables and a thick creamy sauce of parsley, olive oil, vinegar, fresh breadcrumbs, capers and anchovy are built up to pyramid proportions and the outside is decorated in a fantasy of crustaceans. A traditional ingredient that betrays the origins of this now aristocratic concoction is *musciame*, strips of dried dolphin that Genoese sailors used to prepare and eat aboard ship. It can still be bought on the waterfront at Genova. *Bottarga*, pressed, sun-dried fish eggs is another of its classical components. This is an obviously complicated and costly project, in terms of time and ingredients, but there is no reason once you get the basic inspiration not to do as the ancient mariners and build on your own tastes and possibilities. It is a stunning presentation for a buffet table and when Maria's arrived there was a round of spontaneous applause from the delighted feasters.

Another ancient fish specialty of Genova is *baccalà* and *stoccafisso*, two types of dried cod. This may seem strange for a region with a supply of fresh fish right off its shore and even more so because cod is a fish not found in

Santa Margherita Ligure from above

nutritious food that could be preserved for a lengthy period in days when both transportation and refrigeration were difficult.

Although in Italy the names *baccalà* and *stoccafisso* are often used indiscriminately, they are dried in two different ways, and also have different tastes and textures. *Baccalà* is salted and then partially dried, while *stoccafisso*, or stockfish, is unsalted and simply air-dried by letting it hang from a stick in the wind. Before cooking they both need to be left under running water for a couple of days but in Italy your grocer usually does that for you. In Liguria both types of dried cod are used in a variety of ways – fried like fritters, stewed in different sauces or cooked as in a recipe Maria gave me, with potatoes, tomatoes and green olives.

Every June 24, on the feast day of Genova's patron saint, John the Baptist, which also happens to be her nameday, Giovanna opens her summer residence in Portofino for the season with another celebration. It was on this occasion that I asked Maria her secret for making pesto. During that weekend Giovanna served it in its two most classical ways. In *minestrone genovese*, a melody of greens made with fresh lettuce, borage, parsley, chard, leeks, courgettes (zucchini), peas, artichokes, string beans, to which pesto is added at the last minute, more as a seasoning than an ingredient.

Pesto is one of the best imaginable sauces on all types of pasta, particularly for summer meals. It is added cold, of course, while the pasta is steaming hot and then mixed in. The kind of pasta it most traditionally accompanies in Liguria is *trenette*, very thin ribbons of dough, and Maria pours it over elegant little squares of pasta called *lasagnette*.

A final hint about pesto: it keeps its fragrance and flavor remarkably well even in the freezer. I always put away a generous supply so that I can enjoy the aroma and taste of springtime on the Riviera even during the cold Tuscan winter.

Mediterranean waters. It has been imported to Italy from Scandinavia since the Middle Ages. Nonetheless, it is also a very popular food, as we shall see, among another sea-faring people, the Venetians. Certainly the reasons for its popularity in both Liguria and the Veneto can be traced to the advantages for the inland and mountainous areas of these regions of a highly

Skillfully made, this artichoke pie is flaky and light. I have simplified the process by reducing the sheets of dough to 6 plus 6 instead of the usual 12 plus 12. They must still be rolled transparently thin. The meringue dessert also works well with peaches, and in the winter, pears or apples.

Suggested Wines   Drink a Vermentino with this meal. It is one of Liguria's better whites, straw-green in color, fresh and lively to taste.

TORTA PASQUALINA
Artichoke pie

12 young, tender globe artichokes
juice of 1 lemon
2 garlic cloves
1 handful of borage leaves
4 fl oz/1/2 cup/125 ml extra virgin olive oil
10 oz/1 1/4 cups/300 g ricotta cheese
4 oz/1 cup/125 g grated Parmesan cheese
8 eggs
10 oz/2 cups/300 g plain (all-purpose) flour
salt and pepper

Discard the artichoke leaves, chokes and any stems. Slice the hearts and leave them to soak in water with the lemon juice for several minutes. Drain well before cooking.

Chop the garlic and borage. Heat 2 tbsp of the oil in a saucepan, add the artichokes, garlic and borage and cook over low heat. Add salt and pepper, mix in the ricotta, Parmesan and 1 egg and set aside.

Heap the flour on your working surface, make a well in the center and put in half the oil, a pinch of salt and enough water to mix to a medium-soft dough. Divide the dough into 12 parts and roll out each one into 9 in/23 cm round sheets, as thinly as possible.

Brush a spring-clip (springform) pan of the same size with oil. Place 6 layers of dough, brushing each with oil, in the form. Pour in the artichoke mixture. With your finger, make 6 holes in the mixture and break an egg into each one. Cover with another 6 layers of pasta, each brushed with oil.

Beat the remaining egg and brush the surface of the pie. Cook in the oven at 350°F/180°C/Mark 4 for about 1 hour until golden. Serve immediately.

BACCALÀ ALLE OLIVE
Dried cod with potatoes

1 lb/450 g dried cod
3 large potatoes
1 lb/450 g ripe tomatoes
3 1/2 oz/2/3 cup/100 g green olives
2 cloves garlic
1 onion
1 carrot
1 celery stalk
4 fl oz/1/2 cup/125 ml extra virgin olive oil
2 oz/1/4 cup/50 g pine nuts
1 glass white wine
salt and pepper

Torta pasqualina
Baccalà alle olive

Soak the cod for 2 days in cold water, changing the water occasionally. Drain, dry and cut into bite-size pieces. Peel the potatoes and tomatoes and cut into pieces. Stone (pit) the olives, and chop the garlic, onion, carrot and celery.

Heat the oil in a frying pan and stir-fry the garlic, onion, carrot and celery over moderate heat until beginning to brown. Add the cod, tomatoes and potatoes, cover and cook for about 20 minutes, stirring gently once or twice. Add the olives, pine nuts and wine, season with salt and pepper and cook for another 10 minutes. Arrange on a platter and serve.

ALBICOCCHE MERINGATE
Apricot meringues

18 apricots
1 glass sweet white wine
4 oz/½ cup/125 g sugar
5 tbsp raspberry jam
3 egg whites
3 tbsp icing (confectioners') sugar
7 tbsp whipping cream

Stone (pit) the apricots without opening them completely. Close the apricots and cook them in a covered saucepan over low heat with the wine and sugar. Drain the apricots and reduce the cooking juices together with the raspberry jam. Let the apricots and their juices cool completely.

Beat the egg whites together with the icing (confectioners') sugar into firm peaks. Pour a little into 6 small molds. Place 3 apricots in each mold, pour over some of the apricot cooking juices, some whipping cream, and top with the rest of the egg white.

Bake in the oven at 375°F/190°C/Mark 5 for about 20 minutes until they turn light gold. Serve immediately.

MENU FOR A NAME'S DAY

MINESTRONE ALLA GENOVESE
Genoese minestrone

CONIGLIO RIPIENO
Stuffed rabbit

FAGIOLINI IN FRICASSEA
Fricassee of green beans

UOVA ALLA NEVE
Meringues on lemony cream

I particularly enjoy this recipe for minestrone because it is not thickened with rice, pasta or dried beans. The vegetables can, of course, be varied according to the season, but keep all the ingredients green. And cook very slowly for a very long time – certainly not less than 2 hours – so that all the flavors can blend. Do not be put off the stuffed rabbit recipe by the boning process: you can always ask the butcher to do it for you. The dessert is one of those ancient recipes about whose origins there is the usual Italian or French? dispute. I remember that when I was a child our cook made it with a chocolate cream.

Suggested Wines Serve a young Rossese di Dolceacqua, a Ligurian red as pretty as its name, bright ruby in color with the scent of crushed flowers and the flavor of wild berries.

MINESTRONE ALLA GENOVESE
Genoese minestrone

1 onion
2 oz/⅔ cup/50 g pancetta
5 fl oz/⅔ cup/150 ml extra virgin olive oil
1 handful dried porcini mushrooms
1 celery stalk
1 head Boston lettuce
1 handful borage leaves
1 handful parsley
7 oz/200 g Swiss chard
2 leeks
3½ oz/¾ cup/100 g shelled peas
2 courgettes (zucchini)
2 globe artichokes
3½ oz/100 g green beans
60 oz/7½ cups/1.7 liters water
1 handful basil leaves
salt and pepper

Chop the onion and the pancetta and stir-fry with 2 tablespoons of the oil in a large saucepan. Soak the mushrooms in water for about 30 minutes. Drain, squeeze dry and chop. Roughly chop all the other ingredients except the basil, and add them with the mushrooms to the pan, mix well, and pour in the water. Bring to the boil, then cook for about 2 hours over very low heat.

Finely chop the basil and mix with the rest of the oil. Pour the minestrone into a soup tureen, add the basil mixture, stir and serve.

CONIGLIO RIPIENO
Stuffed rabbit

3 lb/1½ kg unboned rabbit
3½ oz/100 g pancetta
2 eggs
2 tbsp chopped marjoram
2 tbsp extra virgin olive oil
3½ oz/ 100 g mortadella, thinly sliced
1 oz/2 tbsp/25 g butter
1 glass white wine
salt and pepper

Bone the rabbit. Lay it out flat, boned side up, and cover with pancetta slices. Beat the eggs on a plate, add salt, pepper and marjoram and mix well.

Oil a large nonstick frying pan, heat well and add eggs; they should cover the bottom in a thin layer. Cook until set and transfer them on top of the pancetta. Layer the mortadella on

Coniglio ripieno e fagiolini in fricassea

top and roll up the rabbit, beginning from the tail end to the head. Tie the thick roll firmly. Place in a casserole with the rest of the oil and the butter. Add salt and pepper.

Cook in the oven at 350°F/180°C/Mark 4 for 1½ hours, basting occasionally with the white wine. Untie, slice and arrange on a platter. Deglaze the cooking juices with a little water, pour over the rabbit and serve.

FAGIOLINI IN FRICASSEA
Fricassee of green beans

1½ lb/700 g green beans
2 tbsp extra virgin olive oil
1 egg yolk
juice of 1 lemon
2 tbsp white wine
salt and pepper

Cook the beans until *al dente* in a pan of boiling, salted water. Run quickly under cold water, drain and return to the pan, together with the oil. Cover and let the flavors merge for a few minutes over a low heat. Season with salt and pepper.

Mix the egg yolk with the lemon juice, white wine and a little seasoning. Pour over the beans and stir for a few seconds to thicken the sauce, without boiling. Arrange the beans around the rabbit and serve.

UOVA ALLA NEVE
Meringues on lemony cream

6 eggs, separated
8 oz/2 cups/225 g icing (confectioners') sugar
36 oz/4½ cups/1 liter milk
vanilla pod (bean)
14 oz/1¾ cups/400 g sugar
grated peel and juice of ½ lemon

Beat the egg whites with the icing (confectioners') sugar to firm peaks. In a large saucepan lightly simmer the milk with the vanilla pod.

Wet a serving spoon with cold water and scoop up a spoonful of the meringue. With the blade of a knife, form it into the shape of a large egg and slide it into the simmering milk. Continue in this way until the meringue is used up. Cook the meringues for a minute on one side, then gently turn and cook for another minute. Drain, spaced well apart on the working surface, and reserve the milk.

Pour the yolks into a saucepan with half the granulated sugar and beat until they thicken. Add 18 fl oz/2¼ cups/500 ml of the milk and the lemon peel, and cook in a double boiler until the cream thickens, without boiling. Pour the cream onto a deep serving platter and cool. Arrange the meringues on top.

In a pan over low heat, dissolve the remaining sugar with the lemon juice until caramelized. Drizzle in an even stream over the meringues and refrigerate until ready to serve.

MENU FOR A RIVIERA REPAST

LASAGNETTE AL PESTO
Small lasagne with pesto sauce

COSTOLETTE DI TONNO
Breaded tuna steaks

PISELLI ALLA GENOVESE
Peas and artichokes with prosciutto

CROSTATA DI FICHI E LIMONI
Fresh fig and lemon tart

The region's restaurants prepare this pasta using large layers of lasagne, usually three, spread with pesto. Lasagnette are a more elegant, family way of presenting this dish. Trout and sole are also good when breaded like the tuna steaks.

For the tart, be sure to use small, sweet figs with thin skins.

Suggested Wines Pigato from the Ligurian Riviera is a full-bodied white that would be delicious with this meal.

LASAGNETTE AL PESTO
Small lasagne with pesto sauce

10½ oz/2 cups/300 g plain (all-purpose) flour
3 eggs
6 tiny basil plants, about 4 in/10cm high
2 garlic cloves
1 tbsp grated pecorino cheese
2 tbsp grated Parmesan cheese
4 fl oz/½ cup/125 ml extra virgin olive oil
1 tbsp pine nuts
salt

Put the flour in a mound on the working surface. Make a well in the center and break the eggs into it. Add a pinch of salt and proceed to make the pasta dough (as explained on page 188.)

Roll out the dough into a thin sheet, and cut into 3 in/10 cm squares. Pick the leaves off the basil plants and purée them in a food processor together with some salt, the garlic, pecorino, Parmesan, olive oil and pine nuts until creamy.

Drop the lasagnette into a pan of salted, boiling water and cook until they rise to the surface. Drain, pour the pesto sauce on top, mix well and serve.

COSTOLETTE DI TONNO
Breaded tuna steaks

4 oz/1 cup/125 g fine dry breadcrumbs
3 tbsp chopped marjoram
finely chopped peel of ½ lemon
1 egg
6 tuna steaks, 1½ in/4 cm thick
4 fl oz/½ cup/125 ml extra virgin olive oil
salt

In a bowl, mix together the breadcrumbs, marjoram and lemon peel. Beat the egg in another bowl with a pinch of salt.

Dip the tuna steaks in the egg batter, coat well with breadcrumbs and fry in the oil for about 2 minutes on each side until lightly browned. Drain on paper towels, arrange on a platter and serve.

PISELLI ALLA GENOVESE
Peas and artichokes with prosciutto

3 globe artichoke hearts
2 oz/⅓ cup/50 g prosciutto chopped
2 tbsp extra virgin olive oil
14 oz/3½ cups/400 g shelled peas
½ glass white wine
1 small head lettuce, shredded
salt

Clean and thinly slice the artichoke hearts. Stir-fry the prosciutto in the olive oil for a couple of minutes. Add the peas and artichoke hearts and salt. Mix well, pour in the wine, cover and cook for 10 minutes over low heat. Add the shredded lettuce, mix again, continue to cook for a couple of minutes, arrange on a platter and serve.

CROSTATA DI FICHI E LIMONI
Fresh fig and lemon tart

7 oz/1½ cups/200 g plain (all-purpose) flour
1 egg yolk
8 oz/1 cup/225 g sugar
3½ oz/3½ tbsp/100 g butter
6 lemons
2¼ lb/1 kg figs, washed, skins left on
1 tsp fennel seeds

Put the flour in a mound on the working surface. Make a well in the center and pour in the egg, half the sugar and the butter. Make a short pastry dough (as explained on page 188.)

Perforate the skins of the lemons all over with a fork, then boil them in water for a couple of minutes. Repeat the boiling process 3 times, changing the water each time. Drain and slice finely, leaving on the skins. Put the lemon slices in a saucepan with the remaining sugar and half a glass of water. Cover and cook over low heat for about 10 minutes. Drain off the syrup and reserve.

Roll out the dough and use to line a buttered and floured tart pan with a removable bottom. Cover the dough with the lemon slices. Slice the figs and arrange on top. Pour the lemon syrup over the figs, sprinkle with the fennel seeds and bake in the oven at 350°F/180°C/Mark 4 for about 45 minutes. Cool, remove from the pan and serve on a platter.

Crostata di fichi e limoni
Lasagnette al pesto

LOMBARDIA

CA'MERA A VARESE

Restoring ancient dishes at the country house of Milanese antiquarian Alessandro Orsi and his wife Lidia

Milano is one of those places abandoned by its inhabitants on weekends and invaded by the population of its endless suburbs in search of big city excitement. Over the years, whenever I have had the bad luck to be stuck there at the end of the week, I flee to the nearby country home of my friends, Lidia and Alessandro Orsi. Ca'Mera, less than an hour's drive from the center of Milano, overlooks the lake of Varese and (on a clear day) one can see the Alps beyond. This area is the entrance to Lombardia's celebrated Lake District, a haven within Italy's most populous and industrialized region, that for centuries has been the retreat of Milanesi from the relatively frenzied life of their city. Once one finally succeeds in leaving the factories behind, the industrial landscape changes amazingly abruptly to one of verdant prealpine hills, fields with well cultivated orchards and vineyards and

Lake Como and above, Ca'Mera from the garden

45

Milan as seen from the gothic Duomo

enchanting villas with terraced gardens encircling the lake.

This particular weekend Lidia has invited me to Ca'Mera to help her to do some "restoration work" on several old dishes from Lombardia, in this case, not plates from Alessandro's collection – he is an international authority on seventeenth-century Italian porcelain and one of Italy's most distinguished antiquarians – but old family recipes. It seems that a few months ago, while cleaning out some cupboards in Milano, she came across several hand-copied recipe books that had belonged to her grandmother, the "grande gourmande" of the family, according to Lidia. Unfortunately, the housekeeper arrived first and had already disposed of a box full but Lidia managed to salvage the rest and it is from these that we are going to work.

Milano and indeed all of Lombardia are perhaps the best places in Italy to discover authentic and ancient regional recipes, still reliably prepared in homes and in the more conscientious restaurants. Paradoxically, this certainly is due to the fact that they are the Italian city and region which have been most assailed from the outside, by immigration from the South and by invaders from the North of Europe. As a result, the Lombardi rather jealously guard the genuineness of their culinary tradition. This is also the wealthiest area of Italy and the upper classes had the money and time to develop and enjoy a refined local cuisine. At the beginning of the nineteenth century, Stendhal, who adored Milano, wrote in his diary that it was "two centuries ahead of Paris in the art of enjoying life." The recipes of Lidia's grandmother come from this very same period and culinary tradition.

It will not be the first time that Lidia and I have collaborated in reviving things from the past. We were once partners in an antique shop specializing in art deco. My husband and I have known Lidia and Sandro since our university days in Milano. We frequented the same *latteria* on via Bagutta. In those days a *latteria* or "milk bar" was a notch below a trattoria on the price index of Italian eateries and Latteria di Betty was our favorite gathering spot. (Some forty-five years later we still meet there to eat but now it has become one of Milano's most popular restaurants.) We married about the same time and our children grew up together. Their three sons, like their father, are now all in the antique business. Then, several years ago when we moved into our pied-à-terre on via Bagutta, we also became neighbors.

Ca'Mera, the Orsi country house, was born a stately Northern Italian aristocrat, tall and slender, sophisticated yet simple. Its burnt-gold stone walls stand dignified and gracious above the bright blue waters of the lake. It is surrounded by several acres of park and gardens and on this splendid site our children used to stage their summer "Olympic Games," racing in and out between the Grecian style statues that grace the garden and doing dare-devil dives into the pool, and – we hope – our grandchildren will soon be doing the same.

When Sandro bought Ca'Mera many years ago, after his heart had been set on it for over three years, it had been reduced to practically a ruin. He began restoration work immediately and this labor of love progressed over the years

Display of antiquarian oddities, Ca'Mera

First-floor gallery, Ca'Mera

(according to the ups and downs of the market for seventeenth-century porcelain!) His dedication and energy for the task, however, never went into slump and the results are stunning.

The original structure was built in the late fifteenth century. The date, 1495, is inscribed on one of the large doors that opens on to an ancient arcade. To its right is the coat of arms of one of those ubiquitous Medici, this time a Milanese "cousin," Pope Pius IV, the uncle of one of the great figures of Milanese history, San Carlo Borromeo, who is buried in the

Duomo. (The present head of the family, Prince Carlo Borromeo, is the owner of Isola Bella on nearby Lake Maggiore.) Additions to the house were built in the seventeenth and nineteenth centuries and it is characteristic of Sandro's aesthetics that he decided to eliminate completely that latter accretion. It is also indicative of his character that wherever possible he reincorporated the ancient building materials into the reconstruction or hunted down others from the same period.

Even more, Sandro's personality permeates

Ca'Mera's pleasing succession of antechambers, grand salons, dining room and library where a casual and comfortable elegance pervades. The furniture is seventeenth- and eighteenth-century, Northern Italian and domestic in style. Many have been the wintry weekends when Lidia and I have gathered couches and armchairs around one of the house's several ancient stone fireplaces and worked away at our knitting. Sandro's selection of paintings and other objects of art is eclectic, almost whimsical but never frivolous or purely decorative. There is a Canaletto alongside a favorite engraving of mostly sentimental value, and a whole kennel of canine portraits, including a massive one of a handsome hound painted in the seventeenth century. Even the two jolly portraits of young Venetian women dressed for *carnevale* that adorn either side of the fine sixteenth-century Lombardo fireplace are of interest for the history of seventeenth-century costume. And the magnificent eighteenth-century Chinese screen that dominates the opposite wall is evocative of the taste of the Lombardo gentry of those times. Yet the overall effect is the opposite of a museum but instead that of a much-loved and lived-in home where now three generations of family and friends enjoy its comforts and beauty. It is the perfect ambience for spending a weekend restoring those "antique plates" of Lidia's grandmother.

Our first dish, an antipasto of capon salad with walnuts, does not really require any restoration. At first glance, in fact, it might seem fresh from the recent *nouvelle cuisine* epoch. Instead, a notation in the margin of the manuscript says it is eighteenth-century in origin and comes from Mantova. The first time I tasted a similar rendition of these ingredients was at Franco Colombani's celebrated restaurant, Il Sole in Maleo near Milano. There is also a classic Lombardo recipe of capon stuffed with a walnut mix and simmered until tender. The traditional Milanese dish for Christmas Eve, and what I also serve my family in Chianti for that feast, is capon *a lesso*, gently boiled with the usual Italian *aromi*, onion, carrot, celery, for an hour and a half to two hours, depending on the weight, until it practically melts in your mouth. That, in fact, is the advantage of capon over other fowl, its exquisite tenderness. It seems that the Romans were the first to discover that a castrated male chicken has the tenderest flesh and the Milanese predilection for this meat could go back to Roman times. Don't forget, Milano was ancient Mediolanum, for almost a century

the capital of the late Roman empire.

So carefully has the recipe for our second dish been handed down from generation to generation of Milanese that it, too, needs no restoration. In her book, *Vecchia Milano in Cucina*, the distinguished historian of the cooking of Lombardia, Ottorina Perna Bozzi, gives four recipes for *risotto giallo* or *alla milanese* (risotto the Milanese way, that is, seasoned with saffron) that span almost two hundred years and nothing has changed from the way I make it today. It is a recipe that has literally been perfected, and the Milanese have certainly had time enough to do so. Rice has been a staple of their diet since the fifteenth century when the Third Duke of Milano, Galeazzo Maria Sforza, introduced it into his Duchy. Over the years they have come up with many ways to flavor it (even with the frogs they catch in the rice fields that stretch for miles around their city) but seasoned with saffron (a delicacy probably introduced during the Spanish occupation), it has become the Milanese first course *par excellence*. The recipe of Lidia's grandmother calls for pumpkin which gives the risotto an appealing sweetness.

In my memories it is associated with another venerable institution of our city. When I was a little girl, the best treat my father could give me was to take me with him to a performance at La Scala. We had a family box that had a little sitting room all decorated in red and gold with a table and an elegant gilded mirror. During the interval a waiter would serve steaming hot *risotto giallo* and my father would let me have a glass of champagne. I cannot remember it ever tasting any better than on those occasions.

Abroad, the most renowned Milanese dish must be *costoletta milanese*, often called in the English-speaking world, breaded veal chop. In the Germanic countries, a bastardized version goes under the name of *Wiener schnitzel*. Now here is a dish that badly needs restoring, which, considering its age (it appears on the menu for a dinner the abbot of the monastery of

Sant'Ambrogio gave in 1134,) is understandable. The authentic dish has nothing in common with that "slice of nondescript meat encased in a sodden jacket of bread and blotting paper," as Elizabeth David so inimitably described the usual English concoction, nor with the Viennese version fried in lard. Properly prepared, it is, I think, one of the world's great, uncomplicated dishes. Lidia's recipe is an ancient variation that adds a bit of zest to this classic. The chops are cooked in a sweet and sour sauce of sugar, raisins and red wine vinegar.

This is another dish of which I have fond childhood memories. Our family cook used to serve the chops with a little paper curicue at the end of each bone. These traditional decorations originally had the function of keeping the grease off dainty fingers but I used them to play with during what seemed like endless adult table conversation.

Although it is true that Italians normally finish their meal with cheese and fruit rather than with a sweet, there is a kind of double cream cheese from Lombardia that is more often than not served as a dessert. Because of its delicate flavor and creamy texture, mascarpone combines particularly well with other foods. *Torte di formaggio* are the newly popular cheese cakes in which it is layered with fresh basil, nuts, and provolone or gorgonzola cheese. These are delicious with fruit. Mascarpone is a favorite of the Milanese and I buy exquisite ones at Milano's celebrated delicatessen, Peck's, still done up in little muslin packets. This cheese, which comes from nearby Lodi, has ancient origins. Casanova mentions in his memoirs that when passing through this area in pursuit of other pleasures, he satisfied his appetite, temporarily at least, with a bowl full of mascarpone. It also appears on the menu of a nobleman's wedding banquet held at Cremona in 1525.

Mascarpone is the featured ingredient in several classic desserts from Lombardia, including *dolce del principe*, a sweet fit for a prince,

which is a kind of creamy trifle. It is, however, delicious just by itself, sprinkled with sugar or powdered chocolate or with a liquor (cognac and rum are traditional) whipped in. My children always liked it spread on bread with jam as an after-school snack. Lidia's grandmother has copied down a recipe in her book that we are going to serve this evening, mascarpone pudding with a hot aniseed sauce. I particularly like the combination of sweet and sour. It cuts down on the richness of the dessert and encourages second helpings!

Because we are many at Ca'Mera this weekend – the Orsi family, children and grandchildren and my eldest son, Paolo, with Roberta and their son, Giacomo, my first grandchild – all come together to enjoy this special Saturday night supper, Lidia has decided to serve it in Sandro's "Wunderkammer" or "chamber of wonders." Here, in the best tradition of an eighteenth-century gentleman-scholar, Sandro has gathered together the "curiosities" of his collection. He has mixed objects of art with items of scientific and naturalistic interest. There are ancient instruments, fossils and minerals and a large stuffed crocodile that scampers up the fireplace wall – much to the delight of every new generation of children.

On the following day, before reluctantly returning to Milano – we must leave early to avoid the heavy traffic heading back into the city from the lakes – Lidia and I gather herbs from her lovely garden: mint, sage and bay. She is going to brew a batch of her famous homemade digestive liquors – a peaceful way to spend a lazy Sunday morning. The process is simple, consisting mainly of soaking the herbs in grain alcohol and setting it aside to age. I am going to take a bottle or two back home to Coltibuono, where, in a few months' time, we hope to taste the result of our efforts and drink together to old friendships, tried and true.

Antiquarian objects include a beautiful Madonna and Child and numerous early globes of the world

49

The capon salad is simple and so elegant served in crystal goblets, that I even put them on the table before my guests take their places. This also saves a trip to the kitchen if you do not have help serving the meal.

A light meat dish served with a vegetable mold was a typical offering at the evening meal in my family. The vegetable was varied from menu to menu. Today I find the combination makes a satisfying main course for supper, especially as the sweetbreads are quite rich.

As an alternative to the aniseed, a hot berry sauce equally complements the mascarpone, and the colors contrast beautifully.

Suggested Wines A fine, flowery white Lugana with the capon salad and a Riviera del Garda red with the main course. Lombardia also makes an exquisite wine with the muscat grape called Moscato di Scanzo, perfect with this region's desserts.

INSALATA DI PETTO DI CAPPONE
ALLE NOCI
Capon salad with walnuts

1 carrot, chopped
1 outer green celery stalk, chopped
1 handful parsley
1 bay leaf
1 capon breast or chicken breast
2 tbsp raisins
1 stalk pale celery heart
6 lettuce leaves
1 tbsp lemon juice
3 tbsp olive oil
8 walnuts, shelled and chopped
salt

Prepare a broth with the carrot, green celery, parsley and bay leaf and 20 fl oz/2½ cups/500 ml water. Simmer for about 30 minutes. Add salt and the capon breast. Cook on a low simmer until just done. Drain and cut into julienne strips when cool.

Soak raisins in water for 30 minutes and drain. Cut the celery stalk into fine julienne strips. Wash and dry the lettuce leaves. Mix celery, capon and raisins together.

Mix together the lemon and oil with a pinch of salt. Arrange the lettuce in 6 goblets and put into each one some of the capon, celery and raisins. Season with the oil and lemon mixture. Decorate with the nuts and serve.

SFORMATO DI CAROTE E SPINACI
Spinach and carrot mold

2 oz/4 tbsp/50 g butter
3¼ oz/⅔ cup/100 g plain (all-purpose) flour
12 fl oz/1½ cups/350 ml milk
1 lb/450 g carrots
2¼ lb/1 kg spinach
½ tsp grated nutmeg
5 oz/1¼ cups/150 g grated Parmesan cheese
4 eggs
salt and pepper

Make a thick béchamel with the butter, flour and milk. Separately cook the carrots and spinach in boiling salted water, drain and purée each through a food mill or food processor.

Add the carrots to half the béchamel and the spinach to the rest. Divide the nutmeg, three-quarters of the Parmesan and the eggs between carrot and spinach mixtures. Add salt and pepper. Mix well, then pour the two vegetable mixtures in layers in a buttered 9 in/23 cm round mold coated with remaining Parmesan.

Place the mold in a larger pan, pour in 1 in/2.5 cm of water and bake in a preheated oven at 350°F/180°C/Mark 4 for about 1 hour. Unmold onto a platter and arrange the sweetbreads around it. Serve immediately.

ANIMELLE AL MARSALA
Sweetbreads in Marsala

2¼ lb/1 kg sweetbreads
2 tbsp plain (all-purpose) flour
2 oz/4 tbsp/50 g butter
4 fl oz/½ cup/125 ml Marsala
8 fl oz/1 cup/225 ml beef broth (page 189)

Cover the sweetbreads with water, bring to a boil and cook for 5 minutes. Drain, rinse under cold water, remove the fat and connecting tubes and cut into bite-size pieces.

Flour the sweetbreads and fry in the butter until they begin to color. Pour in the Marsala. Add the broth a little at a time, cover and cook for 30 minutes over low heat until done. Serve with the vegetable mold.

Sformato di carote e spinaci

MASCARPONE CON SALSA AL SAMBUCO
Mascarpone cheese with hot aniseed sauce

1 1/3 lb/600 g mascarpone cheese
10 oz/2 1/2 cups/300 g aniseed
3 1/2 oz/1/2 cup/100 g sugar
grated peel of 1 lemon

Put the mascarpone in a bowl and stir with a wooden spoon to a creamy consistency. Divide among six goblets and refrigerate.

Put the aniseed in a saucepan with the sugar and the lemon peel and cook over low heat for about 30 minutes, stirring frequently. Pour through a strainer and reheat. Pour the hot aniseed sauce over the mascarpone and serve.

MENU FOR ENJOYING OLD FRIENDS

MINESTRA DI RISO E FILETTO
Rice soup with fillet of beef

FARAONA ARROSTO
Roast guinea fowl (hen)

INVOLTINI DI VERZA
Cabbage rolls

BUDINO DI PESCHE ALLA MENTA
Peach pudding with mint

In Italian the word for the vegetable dish that accompanies the main course is *contorno*, which comes from the verb "to surround," because in families, at least, the main course was served on a platter surrounded by the cooked vegetables, not in a separate plate or bowl as is often now the case. I still serve my *contorni* "surrounding" ("separately" reminds me of a restaurant) and in this menu the color and shape of the cabbage rolls set off nicely the crispy brown of the roast guinea fowl (hen).

Suggested Wines Drink a distinguished red Colle del Calvario, a blend of Merlot and Cabernet Sauvignon from the alpine foothills of Lombardia.

MINESTRA DI RISO E FILETTO
Rice soup with fillet of beef

60 oz/7½ cups/1.7 liters meat broth (see page 189)
7 oz/1 cup/200 g Arborio rice
5 oz/150 g beef fillet
1 tbsp chopped parsley

Bring to a boil 50 oz/6¼ cups/1.4 liters of broth, pour in the rice and cook for 17 minutes. Meanwhile, boil the rest of the broth in another pan.

Cut the beef into pieces the size of toothpicks, then boil in the broth for 1 minute. Drain, add to the rice, sprinkle with parsley and serve.

FARAONA ARROSTO
Roast guinea fowl

1 guinea fowl (hen)
1 lemon
2 oz/4 tbsp/50 g butter
½ glass white wine
salt and pepper

Clean the bird and stuff with the whole lemon. Rub the outside with half the butter, and season with salt and pepper. Cook in a roasting pan with the rest of the butter for 2 hours at 325°F/170°C/Mark 3, basting frequently with a brush.

Remove from the oven and place on a warm dish. Draw off the fat from the roasting pan, then make a sauce by deglazing the pan with the wine and a couple of tablespoons of water. Cut the guinea fowl (hen) into pieces, arrange on a platter, pour over the sauce and serve with the cabbage rolls.

INVOLTINI DI VERZA
Cabbage rolls

12 cabbage leaves
5 oz/⅔ cup/150 g minced (ground) pork
5 oz/⅔ cup/150 g minced (ground) beef
5 oz/150 g pork sausages
2 oz/1½ cup/50 g soft fresh breadcrumbs, soaked in water and squeezed dry
1 egg
3½ oz/scant 1 cup/100 g grated Parmesan cheese
1 sprig thyme
2 oz/4 tbsp/50 g butter
salt

Blanch the cabbage leaves for 1 minute in salted water. Drain, lay them flat on a cloth and press lightly on the stalks.

Mix the meats with the skinned sausages, breadcrumbs, egg, Parmesan and thyme. Place a small portion of this mixture in the center of each leaf, fold over the 2 sides, roll up and secure with a toothpick.

Melt the butter in a frying pan and cook the rolls over low heat for about 20 minutes, turning carefully and moistening occasionally with a little water. Serve with the guinea fowl.

BUDINO DI PESCHE ALLA MENTA
Peach pudding with mint

6 peaches
4 fl oz/½ cup/125 ml sweet white wine
20 mint leaves
8 oz/1 cup/225 g sugar
2 tbsp powdered (unflavored) gelatine
8 fl oz/1 cup/225 ml whipping cream

Drop the peaches into a pan of boiling water for a couple of seconds, then peel. Halve the peaches and slice finely. Cook for about 20 minutes over low heat with the wine, mint leaves and sugar. Remove from heat. Discard the mint leaves if desired and gently mash the peaches with a fork. Dissolve the gelatine, add, and mix in well. Set aside to cool.

Whip the cream until firm, add the peach purée and pour into a wet mold. Refrigerate for at least 4 hours before serving. (Place a hot wet cloth on top of the mold to help turn it out onto a serving platter.)

Risotto con la zucca
Faraona arrosto e involtini di verza

MENU FOR A MILANESE MEAL

RISOTTO CON LA ZUCCA
Risotto with pumpkin

COSTOLETTE IN AGRODOLCE
Veal chops in sweet and sour sauce

PORRI AL BURRO VERSATO
Leeks in butter

CHARLOTTE DI FRUTTA
Fresh fruit charlotte

LIQUORI ALLE ERBE
Homemade herbal liqueurs

Risotto must always be creamy and the pumpkin in this recipe makes it even more so, besides adding an attractive sweetness. The rice must remain *al dente* on the inside and Arborio is the only variety that gives this unique consistency to the dish, creamy yet firm to the bite. (My experience of risotto outside Italy is that if it errs, it errs on the side of being too dry.) Leave a little liquid in it at the end of cooking. It will be absorbed when the Parmesan is added and before you get it to the table. And remember that, like pasta, risotto must be served at once.

Suggested Wines Either a Barbera or Pinot Nero from the Oltrepò Pavese zone of Lombardia would be excellent with this meal.

RISOTTO CON LA ZUCCA
Risotto with pumpkin

10 oz/3 cups/300 g cubed raw pumpkin flesh
1 small onion
6 oz/12 tbsp/180 g butter
50 fl oz/6 cups/1.4 liters chicken broth (page 189)
1 glass dry white wine
18 oz/2⅓ cups/500 g Arborio rice

½ tsp powdered saffron
3½ oz/scant 1 cup/100 g grated Parmesan cheese
salt and pepper

Wrap the pumpkin in foil and cook about 30 minutes at 350°F/180°C/Mark 4. Rub through a sieve or purée in a food processor.

Finely chop the onion and cook gently in a frying pan with half the butter until transparent. In a saucepan, bring the broth to the boil and keep at a simmer. Add the rice to the onion, cook for a couple of minutes over moderate heat, stirring frequently. Pour in the wine and allow to evaporate, then add the pumpkin and enough broth to keep the rice covered. Continue adding enough broth to keep the rice covered, stirring constantly. Cook for 10 minutes, then dissolve the saffron powder in 1 tbsp broth and add to the rice.

After a further 5 minutes cooking, turn off the heat, add the remaining butter and the Parmesan, mix and cover for a couple of minutes before pouring into a serving bowl.

COSTOLETTE IN AGRODOLCE
Veal chops in sweet and sour sauce

1 oz/2 tbsp/25 g raisins
6 veal chops, lightly pounded
1 egg, lightly beaten with a little salt on a plate
7 oz/1¾ cups/200 g dry breadcrumbs
3½ oz/7 tbsp/100 g butter
2 tbsp sugar
1 tbsp potato flour (or cornstarch)
8 fl oz/1 cup/225 ml vinegar, red wine and water mixed in equal parts
salt and pepper

Soak the raisins in warm water for 30 minutes and drain. Dip each chop on both sides in the egg and coat with breadcrumbs.

Heat the butter in a heavy frying pan large enough to hold the chops in 1 layer. Add the meat and cook on both sides over moderate

heat until golden. Drain on paper towels and keep warm. Pour off the fat from the pan.

Dissolve the sugar in the pan over moderate heat and mix in the potato flour. When it begins to color add the vinegar mixture, stirring continuously, until it thickens slightly.

Replace the chops side by side in the pan, sprinkle with the raisins and salt and pepper, cover and cook for 5 minutes over low heat. Arrange the chops on a platter, cover with the sauce and serve while hot, surrounded by the leeks.

PORRI AL BURRO VERSATO
Leeks in butter

3½ lb/1.5 kg medium-sized leeks
3½ oz/7 tbsp/100 g butter
2 oz/½ cup/50 g grated Parmesan cheese
salt and pepper

To facilitate cleaning, make a cut lengthwise through the leeks, from the white end to the green tip. Turn each 90° and repeat. Wash well, cook in boiling salted water for about 10 minutes and drain.

Heat the butter, put the leeks on a serving dish, sprinkle with the Parmesan, season and pour over the butter and serve.

CHARLOTTE DI FRUTTA
Fresh fruit charlotte

For the short pastry:
12 oz/2½ cups/350 g plain (all purpose) flour
2 egg yolks
4 oz/½ cup/125 g sugar
8 oz/16 tbsp/225 g butter
salt
For the filling:
1 orange
10 oz/300 g plums

2 lb/1 kg apples

8 oz/1 cup/225 g sugar

grated peel of 1 lemon

2 tbsp Marsala

3 cloves

1 vanilla pod (bean)

Prepare the short pastry dough using the flour, egg yolks, sugar, butter and pinch of salt (page 188). To make the filling, grate the peel of the orange and reserve. Peel the orange, removing any pith, and divide into segments. Peel the plums and apples and cut into pieces. Cook the fruit together with the sugar, the lemon and orange peel, Marsala, cloves and vanilla pod for about 20 minutes over low heat.

Roll out two-thirds of the short pastry dough and use it to line a buttered and lightly floured spring-clip (springform) pan. Fill with the cooked fruit and cover with the remaining dough, rolled out thinly. Cook in a preheated oven at 350°F/180°C/Mark 4 for 45 minutes. Let cool slightly before removing from the pan. Serve at room temperature.

LIQUORI ALLE ERBE
Homemade herbal liqueurs

8 oz/1 cup/225 g sugar

8 fl oz/1 cup/225 ml water

8 fl oz/1 cup/225 ml 95% (192°) Grappa

40 leaves lemon verbena or sage, or 30 fresh mint leaves, or the peel of 3 oranges

Put the sugar and alcohol together with the chosen herb or orange peel in a bottle. Cork and shake. Store in a cupboard for 20 days, shaking the bottle well twice daily. Strain the liquid through a paper filter into a clean bottle and the liqueur is ready to drink.

Charlotte di frutta

VENETO

VILLA MARCELLO A LEVADA

Civilized cuisine in the Venetian villa of Count and Countess
Vettor and Carlotta Marcello

There are villas and then there are Villas, and there is something about the Villas of the Veneto that makes all the others seem like poor country cousins. Of course, I am exaggerating, but these most splendid of country residences and the civilization they symbolize really are of a world apart. They were built during the two golden eras of the Republic of Venezia. In the first period, the High Renaissance, Palladio created their neoclassic design and artists of the caliber of Paolo Veronese were commissioned to decorate their interiors. In the second, the age of baroque and rococo, the wealth of centuries of the Venetian Republic, the richest of Europe, was lavished on their expansion, ornamentation and gardens, often small versions of Versailles. The Tiepolo, father and son, glorified their grand rooms with magnificent frescos.

The patrician owners of these villas con-

Giorgione's Castelfranco Veneto, a short distance from Villa Marcello,
and above, a detail of the wonderful ballroom ceiling

structed them on *terra ferma*, as the Venetians still refer to the mainland off their not-so-stable islands, along or near the banks of the several rivers that flow down from the Alps, through the flat, fertile plain of the Veneto and into the Adriatic. This gave them easy access by boat when they felt the need to escape the claustrophobic atmosphere of Venezia. The boats themselves were like elegant floating drawing rooms where the passengers idled away the brief journey playing cards and enjoying gastronomic delicacies. Once arrived they could stretch their legs in ways not possible in Venezia, hunt, ride through the countryside and tend their farms. In fact, these villas had their origins as farming estates and even in the eighteenth century when they had become pleasure palaces, many estates remained serious agricultural enterprises.

From what can be gleaned from the literature and paintings of that era, the daily routine of these holiday residences seems to have consisted of a series of frivolous amusements, games, banqueting and, of course, "sentimental adventures." (Casanova was certainly a frequent visitor to these parts.) Life went on in much this way until the mid-nineteenth century when these grand country houses were for the most part abandoned. Their decaying ornament and overgrown gardens inspired the romantic sense of many a Victorian tourist.

Fortunately, one of the finest, the Villa Marcello at Levada, not only survived the centuries intact, but is now enjoying a third golden age. It is owned by the Marcello family who built it in the sixteenth century as a farm and remodeled it extensively in the eighteenth. (For a very brief period it went out of the family after one member lost it in a game of cards, but was quickly ransomed by a less reckless relative.) They are one of the few Italian dynasties that can claim direct descent from a *gens romana*. During the barbarian invasions of Roma they vanished from the pages of history, only to turn up on the registers of the Republic of Venezia in 983. A thousand years later, in 1983, fifty-three members congregated in the family palace to celebrate their first millennium in Venezia.

Vettor Marcello is the present owner of the villa. When he inherited the estate from his uncle some ten years ago, he and his wife, Carlotta, came to the decision that the only way to do justice to this eminent patrimony was to move there with their two young sons and make it the family home. As romantic as it may seem to call an historical Venetian villa home, it was a decision verging on the courageous. These grand, ancient houses have a life all their own, as well I know, and to live in harmony with them today requires considerable dedication and sacrifice. Vettor and Carlotta, however, are young and dynamic and have combined their energy and talents in this project with intelligence.

Vettor began to modernize both the production and marketing of the six-hundred-acre farm. In addition to vineyards of Chardonnay, Pinot Grigio, Cabernet and Raboso from which he produces some twelve thousand bottles of fine wine, he cultivates tobacco, grain, soya, onions and peaches. His latest addition is a high-tech greenhouse where he raises seventy-thousand house plants.

Carlotta set about renovating the villa. This did not mean giving orders to a squadron of servants but entailed taking scissors in hand to make new damask drapes for the drawing rooms, scrubbing the splendid marble staircases and, more to her liking, studying antique restoration in Venezia. The first time I visited the villa I found her engaged in all-out warfare against the moles that were undermining the formal front lawn. When I later asked how many workers it took to maintain the extensive park and gardens, she broke into a hearty laugh.

Villa Marcello

A teapot from the famous Bassano potteries

The house is well worthy of their labor. The visitor's first view of it, through the ornate wrought-iron entrance gates, is across an immense, symmetrical garden with central fountain, to the gleaming white Palladian-style façade, flanked on both sides by a long, graceful colonnade called *la barchessa*. The interior of the house is alive with Venetian verve and color. The rooms still have their original eighteenth-century furniture and decoration and give continual delight to the eyes. On the first floor is a magnificent ballroom with frescoed ceiling and walls by Giovanni Battista Crosato, who, in his day, was as highly esteemed as his contemporary Tiepolo. Less grand but even more exceptional are the wonderful stuccoes depicting scenes of rural life on the walls of the upstairs bedrooms. They are unique and Carlotta hopes one day to have time to research and write about them.

In the family room above the grand piano where their son Jacopo practices his music lessons is an ancestral portrait of the celebrated baroque composer and musician, Benedetto

Marcello. He wrote the kind of music one could imagine performed in this house. In fact, there is something about the villa, perhaps the harmony of its exterior and the chromatic colors and design of its interiors, that makes one feel that it was made for music. Chamber music was an important event in the cultural life of these Venetian villas and a more congenial setting would be hard to find. In the overall renaissance that Vettor and Carlotta have initiated at Villa Marcello, they are particularly interested in reviving its tradition of music. Their inaugural concert was given by the Solisti Veneti who performed works by Vivaldi.

Afterward, Vettor and Carlotta hosted a candlelight supper served under the arches of *la barchessa*. On the many occasions when they entertain, Carlotta not only directs the work in the kitchen but, when the groups are small, cooks herself. She composes her menus around the classical dishes of the Veneto and fortunately Villa Marcello is in the province of Treviso, which is the most acclaimed in the region for its gastronomy. It is called the "garden of Venezia" and has retained its reputation for fine cooking that began with the doges, who moved to its cooler climate in the summer. The cooking of the Veneto, however, is not the lavish and ornate cuisine one associates with Venezia. After all, one of the reasons these Venetians came out to the country was to take a breather from the extravagances of their exotic capital. Even in the kitchens of the great houses, the cooks prepared simple country dishes – refined, of course, to perfection.

Beans and especially rice are the two humble staples of Veneto cooking. The Veneti make more use of rice than does any other region of Italy. It is said that there is nothing that moves on land, sea or air that has not ended up in one of their rice dishes. First there are marvelous soups in which they combine rice with every available green and vegetable – asparagus tips, celery, leeks, cabbage, lettuce,

fennel, courgettes (zucchini), potatoes, pumpkin, raisins and even hops. The most famous combination, often on the menu at Villa Marcello, is called in Venetian dialect *risi e bisi*, rice and peas. You may well ask what is so special about it, but the way they prepare it here, when done well, does raise these two modest ingredients to a new level. It must be made from very fresh sweet peas, which every restaurateur in Venezia claims were picked that morning from the vegetable fields off the lagoon. Some older recipes even specify that after shelling, the pea pods should be boiled separately in order to flavor the water for the rice. The peas are briefly cooked in pancetta, onion and parsley; the rice is boiled in broth and at the end both are mixed with butter and Parmesan. It should have the consistency of a dense soup and is traditionally eaten with a fork. It is a dish that stands on the culinary border between rice soup and risotto, for the Veneti prefer their risotto more liquid than in the rest of Northern Italy. "*Deve avere l'onda*" – it should be wavy, they say, which is appropriate for a people who so often combine it with fish. I consider risotto and seafood, especially

Rose-covered garden statue

The rear garden of Villa Marcello as seen from the ballroom balcony

northern Adriatic crab whose legs make it resemble a spider. I find it tastier than Atlantic and Pacific crab. It is hard work to get to its meat but the reward is sweet when you do. Carlotta served it as a first course at an elegant benefit buffet supper I attended. She simply dressed its succulent meat with orange peel, lemon juice, parsley, olive oil and pepper and served it in the upper shells.

Polenta is the staple of Veneto cooking. It is also a traditional dish in Piemonte and Lombardia, but there it is made from a coarse, yellow flour. Here a fine, white cornflour from the neighboring Friuli region is used. This gives the Veneto version a more refined appearance as well as taste. It can also be prepared in quite sophisticated ways. Every good cook in a country house will know how to make *pasticcio di polenta* (polenta pie), in which thin slices of polenta alternate with layers of wood pigeon, cheese, ham and mushrooms. It is the inevitable accompaniment to one of the most classical of Venetian dishes, *fegato alla veneziana*, made with the thinnest possible slices of the tenderest calves' liver, cooked on each side for a minute only and served with slices of onion braised golden yellow. Another classical way to prepare polenta is with little game birds, in which these tiny creatures are skewered and pan-roasted and placed on top of a platter of polenta with their cooking juices poured over. I remember that Carlotta served polenta with quail at my first luncheon in Villa Marcello. They had been stuffed with juniper berries, wrapped in pancetta and pan-roasted in butter. On each plate she put a portion of creamy white polenta and placed on top a slice of toast with the quail.

Another ancient specialty of the Veneto that is often served with polenta is *baccalà*, dried cod. As in Liguria, this may seem strange for a region with an ample supply of fresh fish. It was, however, an important source of nourishment in the interior parts of the region, especially on the many days of religious abstinence from meat. In Italy the word *baccalà*

shellfish, one of the happiest marriages in cooking. The list of this coupling in Veneto cuisine seems endless: scampi, mussels, scallops, eel, sea bass, trout, and squid cooked with their ink sacs for *risotto nero* (black rice.) On her list, Carlotta has a recipe for risotto with prawns (shrimp) and celery, another felicitous combination.

She also prepares risotto in a mold, which is a very successful variation of the rice molds that are standard fare in Italian home cooking, although never served in restaurants. Because

the rice for risotto is allowed to absorb the flavors of the broth and vegetables in which it is cooked, it provides a more full-bodied taste in a mold than rice boiled in abundant liquid. There are also occasions when, because of timing or the number of guests, normal risotto would be very difficult or impossible to serve, but when a risotto mold could be prepared in advance.

One shellfish found in the Venetian lagoon so exquisite and rare I would not want to share it even with risotto is *granceola*. This is a is often used for both types of dried cod, one salted (*baccalà,*) and one unsalted and air-dried (*stoccafisso* or stockfish.) In the Veneto it is stockfish that is used in the famous recipe from the province of Vicenza, *baccalà alla vicentina.* The cod must first be softened by soaking for a couple of days. Then it is browned in onion, parsley and some anchovy fillet and left to simmer in milk for four to five hours. When a small group of very prestigious American businessmen with their wives came to luncheon at Villa Marcello, Carlotta racked her brain for hours trying to think of something to serve that their sophisticated palates had not yet savored. She decided on *baccalà* stewed with leeks in white wine, a brilliant example, I think, of humble ingredients refined to perfection.

The Veneti are particularly proud of the produce from their vegetable gardens and with excellent reason. Even in Venezia itself, where you might not expect it, salads are composed of a variety of tasty greens that have been

Bassano del Grappa

Asolo, famous for its June cherry festival, produces wonderful fresh fruit tarts

freshly picked in the fields of the Po delta. In the north of the region Bassano produces a tender white asparagus and Lamon near Belluno a succulent white bean that, fresh or dried, is the principal ingredient in the celebrated Veneto dish known in dialect as *pasta e fasoei,* a thick bean soup made with pork stock and with dry pasta added at the end. Carlotta takes advantage of the abundance of fine, fresh vegetables at the Treviso market in a colorful and uncomplicated way. She serves them as an antipasto vegetable platter, raw with an enriched vinaigrette sauce.

The supreme vegetable of the Treviso market is its prized radicchio. It is also its rarest. The genuine item appears for just a few weeks, usually from the beginning of December. Locally it is referred to as "*un fiore che si mangia,*" an edible flower. It really belongs to the group of root chicories, although only its leaves are eaten. It is easy to see why it is

compared to a flower. It has a long, white stalk and spearlike leaves that are gorgeous ruby-red with white veins. It is crisp, aromatic and has a slight and pleasingly bitter taste. The most typical way to eat it in Treviso is grilled with some of its outer leaves burnt literally to a crisp. Of course, it is delicious on its own in a salad or maybe mixed with another crisp raw vegetable like fennel. Carlotta also bakes it in the oven with olive oil and wine, which is probably the best way to cook radicchio when you have to substitute the Treviso with another red variety.

Another winter vegetable that is popular in the Veneto for its culinary qualities is the yellow pumpkin, *zucca gialla.* Its gnarled yellow-green exterior is not as attractive as the smooth American variety but inside it is sweet and tasty. It is grown in Chioggia, a fishing village on the south side of the Venetian lagoon that is also a garden produce center for the

Veneto. Here the traditional way of preparing pumpkin is to deep-fry slices in olive oil, then to pour over boiling hot vinegar and marinate them for several hours before eating. I remember as a little girl driving with my family through the Veneto countryside that borders on Lombardia and stopping for a roadside snack that consisted of baked pumpkin slices sprinkled with sugar. In Mantova they use it as a stuffing for tortelli. It is perhaps most often prepared as a sweet – pumpkin fritters made with sugar and raisins, pumpkin tarts and even pumpkin preserves. For dessert at a supper following a most memorable chamber concert at Villa Marcello, Carlotta served a creamy pumpkin pudding, made with eggs and amaretti cookies and seasoned with nutmeg.

The desserts I most associate with the elegant households of the Veneto are *coppette*, fruit preparations or ices, and cooked creams served in graceful crystal goblets. Carlotta left me two of these recipes as refined and tasteful as Villa Marcello itself. One is a cup of grapes, cooked with quince and lemon until it is almost gelatin and served topped with whipped cream. The other is zabaglione flavored with strawberries.

It is probable that zabaglione originated here (not in Sicilia, as is commonly held) when some inspired cook added Marsala wine, brought back by the Venetian fleet from Sicilia, to the classic egg-cream. Wherever the notion came from, blended with sweet strawberries and cream from the Veneto, it is an admirable combination of tastes from the north and south of the country.

Evening light on the Valle di Brenta near Chioggia

MENU FOR MR ROCKEFELLER

❧

RISOTTO IN FORMA
Risotto mold

BACCALÀ CON I PORRI
Dried cod with leeks

RADICCHIO AL FORNO
Baked radicchio

CREMA CON LE FRAGOLE
Strawberry zabaglione

The dishes in this menu all have very distinct, attractive flavors. The cod and leeks combine and cook particularly well together; use the fillet of fish, which is the fleshy part. As I have said, risotto should normally be quite liquid at the end of cooking. In this recipe it needs to remain moist, but dry enough to mold.

Those of us who do not live in the Treviso area will have to be content to use the ordinary variety of red radicchio. This is also good sautéd or grilled with olive oil, but baking it in this way makes it less bitter.

The classical Venetian way to make zabaglione is with wild strawberries. If you don't have access to these, try to find the domestic ones with the most intense flavor.

Suggested Wines A menu for whites from the Veneto – a light and fruity Tocai from the Friuli with the risotto, a fuller Breganzo Pinot Bianco with the cod and a sweet Recioto di Soave with dessert.

RISOTTO IN FORMA
Risotto mold

1 green tomato
60 fl oz/7½ cups/1.5 liters chicken broth (page 189)
1 small onion
2 white celery stalks
2 carrots
3½ oz/7 tbsp/100 g butter
1¼ lb/scant 3 cups/600 g Arborio rice
1 glass white wine
3½ oz/scant 1 cup/100 g grated Parmesan cheese
8 courgette (zucchini) flowers, for decoration

Dip the tomato for a couple of seconds in boiling water, peel and dice. Bring the broth to a simmer. Finely chop the onion, cut the celery and carrots into julienne strips.

Stir-fry the onion with half the butter in a saucepan over low heat until it becomes transparent. Add the rice and stir to let it take on flavor for a couple of minutes. Pour in wine and let it cook until it evaporates.

Add the rest of the vegetables, pour in enough of the simmering broth to just cover the rice and continue to cook over moderate heat, adding a ladle of broth whenever necessary to keep the rice covered and stirring constantly. Cook the rice for about 15 minutes, letting it get dry as it finishes. Add the rest of the butter, the Parmesan and mix well.

Put the rice in a buttered ring mold, press down well and bake in a preheated oven for 5 minutes at 375°F/190°C/Mark 5. Unmold onto a serving platter, decorate with the courgette (zucchini) flowers and serve.

Risotto in forma

BACCALÀ CON I PORRI
Dried cod with leeks

1¼ lb/600 g dried cod
2 tbsp plain (all-purpose) flour
6 leeks
2 oz/4 tbsp/50 g butter
4 tbsp extra virgin olive oil
1 glass dry white wine
18 fl oz/2¼ cups/500 ml milk
salt and pepper

Soak the cod in cold water for 2 days, changing the water frequently, to tenderize it and eliminate the salt. Drain the cod and dry well. Cut into serving-size pieces, and coat with flour.

Remove discolored leaves from the leeks, cut off green tops, wash under cold water and slice finely. Place leeks in a large, shallow flameproof casserole, add the cod, butter and olive oil and cook over low heat until the leeks become transparent. Pour in the wine and cook until it evaporates. Add the milk, salt and pepper. Transfer to the oven and bake at 350°F/180°C/Mark 4 for about 2 hours. Transfer to a platter and serve.

RADICCHIO AL FORNO
Baked radicchio

6 heads red radicchio
2 tbsp extra virgin olive oil
2 tbsp white wine
salt and pepper

Remove withered leaves from the radicchio and slice each one lengthwise into two sections.

Grease a baking pan with olive oil, put in the radicchio side by side, add salt, pepper, the rest of the olive oil and the white wine. Bake in the oven at 350°F/180°C/Mark 4 for about 20 minutes. Arrange on a platter and serve.

CREMA CON LE FRAGOLE
Strawberry zabaglione

6 egg yolks
8½ oz/20 tbsp/240 g granulated sugar
8 fl oz/1 cup/225 ml dry Marsala
2 tbsp powdered (unflavored) gelatine
8 fl oz/1 cup/225 ml whipping cream
3 tbsp icing (confectioners') sugar
1¼ lb/600 g strawberries
2 tbsp lemon juice
½ glass white wine

Beat the egg yolks with 6 oz/14 tbsp/180 g of the granulated sugar until creamy. Add the Marsala and place in a double boiler over moderate heat. Continue to beat until the zabaglione thickens. Add the powdered gelatine dissolved in 2 tbsp water. Set aside to cool completely.

Whip the cream with the icing sugar until it forms stiff peaks, and add to the zabaglione. Purée about one-sixth of the strawberries with a food mill or food processor and marinate the rest in a bowl with remaining sugar, the lemon juice and white wine.

Put the zabaglione in a serving bowl, pour over the strawberry purée and refrigerate for at least 3 hours. Serve with the remaining strawberries.

Crema con le fragole

This menu is well suited for a sit-down meal for a large number of guests. The vegetable platter is easy, beautiful and can be varied with the season. The quail are not complicated and the fine, white polenta is more appropriate for formal occasions than the coarser, yellow kind traditional in Lombardia.

Italian pumpkins have a rough surface and their flesh is wonderfully tasty. Use a variety with pronounced flavor for this pudding.

Suggested Wines Drink a light Bardolino rosé with the first course, an elegant Raboso with the quail and, as a dessert wine, Recioto della Valpolicella.

GIARDINIERA DI VERDURE
Garden vegetable platter

1 raw beetroot (beet)
7 oz/200 g green beans
6 ripe tomatoes
1 carrot
2 very fresh courgettes (zucchini)
1 onion
1 cucumber
1 egg yolk
pinch of mustard powder (dry mustard)
1 tbsp red wine vinegar
salt and pepper
4 tbsp extra virgin olive oil

several parsley sprigs
several watercress leaves

Boil the beetroot in lightly salted water until tender. Cook green beans in a pan of salted boiling water for about 10 minutes. Drain both and cool under cold running water.

Dice the tomatoes, and cut the carrot and courgettes (zucchini) into julienne strips. Cut the green beans into small pieces, peel and finely slice the onion and beetroot, and the cucumber with its skin on. Beat the egg yolk together with salt, mustard and vinegar. Add pepper and olive oil and mix well.

Arrange the vegetables in alternating colors on a large serving platter. Decorate with the parsley and watercress, pour over the dressing and serve.

QUAGLIE SUL CROSTONE E POLENTA
Quail on toast with polenta

13 oz/2⅔ cups/375 g polenta flour (fine white cornmeal)
60 fl oz/7½ cups/1.5 liters water
1 tbsp juniper berries
6 quail
6 thin slices pancetta
6 slices good thick bread
2 oz/4 tbsp/50g butter
½ glass white wine
salt and pepper

Pour the polenta flour into a pan of boiling salted water, stirring vigorously with a whisk to prevent lumps forming. Cook for about 40 minutes, stirring occasionally with a wooden spoon. Chop the juniper berries and stuff them inside the quail; add salt and pepper.

Wrap each quail in a slice of pancetta. Cook uncovered in a flameproof casserole over moderate heat with half the butter for about 30 minutes, turning gently from time to time. For the final 10 minutes of cooking, pour in the white wine and cover. When done, discard the pancetta and keep the quail warm.

Quaglie sul crostone e polenta

Giardiniera di verdure

Spread the slices of bread with the rest of the butter and toast in a preheated oven at 350°F/180°C/Mark 4 until golden brown. Divide the polenta among 6 plates, spreading smoothly. Top each serving with a slice of bread and a quail, divided into 2 sections. Serve hot.

BUDINO DI ZUCCA
Pumpkin pudding

1¼ lb/600 g pumpkin, peeled and seeded
4 eggs, separated
5 tbsp sugar
3½ oz/¾ cup/100 g plain (all-purpose) flour
1 tsp baking powder
8 fl oz/1 cup/225 ml milk
6 amaretti biscuits (cookies)
pinch of grated nutmeg

Bake the pumpkin in the oven at 350°F/180°C/Mark 4 until it becomes soft. In a large bowl, beat the yolks of the eggs together with the sugar. Sift the flour and add a little at a time with the baking powder and the milk, taking care that lumps do not form. Pulverize the amaretti in a food processor, add nutmeg and blend into the mixture. Beat the egg whites to firm peaks and carefully blend into the mixture.

Butter and flour a mold, pour in the mixture and bake at 350°F/180°C/Mark 4 for about 1 hour until a toothpick inserted in the center comes out clean. Turn out onto a platter and serve immediately.

MENU FOR AN OUTDOOR CANDLELIGHT BUFFET

GRANCEOLA ALLA SCORZA D'ARANCIA
Spider crabs with orange

PASTICCIO DI FEGATO D'OCA ALLA VENEZIANA
Goose liver pâté Venetian style

INSALATA DI PISELLI
Fresh green pea salad

COPPETTE DI UVA FRAGOLA
Grape cups

The first half of this menu is high on preparation time, but the work can be done well ahead of time and the dishes served cold. *Granceola* (spider crab) in Italy is found only in the Venetian lagoon and considered a delicacy. Use any large crab.

The pâté is a variation on the classical Venetian combination of liver and onions. Homemade pâtés have always been a tradition of the *cucina alto-borghese*. I have tried to simplify the process as much as possible and once learned, it will serve you well. Although there is no substitute for fresh peas, the baby garden variety do seem to be one vegetable that retains flavor even when frozen. *Uva fragola* (strawberry grape) is a particular hybrid (from an American variety) that covers many a pergola in the Veneto and is often used for homemade wine. It has a distinctly strawberry fragrance. Substitute any sweet and scented table variety.

Suggested Wines   Your guests will be more than content to stay with an *abboccato* (semisweet) Prosecco di Conegliano spumante throughout the entire buffet.

Granceola alla scorza d'araneia

GRANCEOLA ALLA SCORZA D'ARANCIA
Spider crabs with orange

6 large fresh crabs
1 orange
juice of 1 lemon
salt and pepper
6 tbsp extra virgin olive oil
1 bunch parsley, chopped

Put the crabs in a pan of salted, boiling water and cook for about 30 minutes.

Discard the bottom shells and delicately scoop out the crabmeat. Clean and set aside the upper shells. Crack open the legs and claws and remove the meat. Use the "butter" (the yellow mass of fat and organs) for another dish.

Grate the peel of the orange and squeeze the juice. Mix together the lemon juice, salt, pepper, olive oil, orange juice and grated peel. Combine with the crabmeat. Fill the emptied shells with the mixture, sprinkle with parsley and serve.

PASTICCIO DI FEGATO D'OCA ALLA VENEZIANA
Goose liver pâté Venetian style

For the gelatine:
2¼ lb/1 kg lean beef
1 pig's trotter (foot)
10 oz/300 g calf's head
1 carrot
1 celery stalk
1 bay leaf
1 bunch parsley
1 chicken breast, roughly chopped
1 tbsp almond oil
For the pâté:
1 lb/450 g onions
10 oz/1¼ cups/300 g butter
1 lb/450 g goose liver, thinly sliced
salt and pepper
2 tbsp Marsala
2 tbsp brandy
2 egg yolks
1 black truffle, sliced

To make the gelatine, boil the beef together with the pig's trotter, calf's head, carrot, celery, bay leaf and parsley in 90 fl oz/ 2½ quarts/2.5 litres water. Cook over low heat for about 4 hours.

Strain the broth in a colander and set aside

to cool. Skim off the fat that forms on the surface. Put the broth in a saucepan, add the pieces of chicken breast and cook for 1¼ hours until transparent, skimming occasionally.

Pour half the broth into a large, shallow pan, chill until it sets and chop into fine dice. Oil a pâté mold and pour in a thin layer of the remaining broth. Refrigerate the mold to form the gelatine.

To make the pâté, slice the onions and stir-fry with half the butter over low heat, without coloring. Add the liver and cook for a few minutes on high heat, keeping inside rare.

Strain off most of the fat and put the liver in a food processor together with salt, pepper, Marsala, brandy, and the rest of the butter (in soft pieces). Process until it has the consistency of thick cream. Put the mixture in a chilled bowl set inside a larger bowl with ice in the bottom. Add the egg yolks and mix with a whisk until it thickens. Spread the pâté in the prepared mold, smooth the surface and pour in the rest of the broth. Refrigerate for at least 3 hours.

Unmold the pâté on to a serving platter, arrange the chopped gelatine around it, garnish with slices of truffle and serve.

INSALATA DI PISELLI
Fresh green pea salad

1¼ lb/5 cups/600 g shelled peas
6 tbsp extra virgin olive oil
salt
1 handful whole almonds
1 tbsp chopped fresh parsley
1 tbsp chopped fresh tarragon

Cook the peas in a pan of salted, boiling water for 5 minutes. Drain, arrange in a salad bowl and season with oil and salt. Roughly chop the almonds.

When the peas have cooled, sprinkle with parsley, tarragon and chopped almonds and serve.

COPPETTE DI UVA FRAGOLA
Grape cups

3 lb/1.5 kg sweet red table grapes
2 quinces
2 fl oz/¼ cup/50 ml red wine
1 whole lemon
10 oz/1¼ cups/300 g sugar
8 fl oz/1 cup/225 ml whipping cream

Set aside several of the grapes for garnish. Put the rest through a food mill to obtain 10 fl oz/ 1¼ cups/300 ml juice.

Cut the quinces into segments, leaving on skins. Place in a saucepan with the wine and the lemon fruit and peel, cover and cook over low heat for about 1 hour, or until very soft. Pour the mixture into a cloth, drain and squeeze out the juice. Add the grape juice and sugar to the quince liquid and cook over low heat for about 30 minutes, skimming the surface, until the liquid becomes transparent.

Toward the end of cooking, test a drop or two on a plate. When it sets almost immediately, pour into 6 crystal cups. Leave to cool. Whip the cream and use to garnish the cups along with the reserved whole grapes.

Pasticcio di fegato d'oca alla veneziana

EMILIA-ROMAGNA

PALAZZO BOSDARI A BOLOGNA

*Food for thought in the home of Count and Countess Giuseppe
and Grazia Gazzoni Frascara*

What is, perhaps, still the most appropriate attitude for a gastronomic visit to Bologna was recommended one hundred years ago by that venerable writer on Italian cuisine, Pellegrino Artusi, in his cookbook classic, *La scienza in cucina e l'arte di mangiar bene* (The Science of Cooking and the Art of Good Eating.) He held that the mere mention of Bolognese cooking "merits a genuflection" and observed that although it is a rich cuisine it is nevertheless a healthy one because so many Bolognesi live to a ripe old age. This combination of richness and well-being, together with the fact that it is the capital of Emilia-Romagna, Italy's most fertile region, earned for Bologna centuries before Artusi its renowned title "*La Grassa*," Bologna the Fat.

The region takes the first half of its name from the ancient Roman road, the Via Emilia, which still traverses it for a hundred and thirty

*Panorama of Bologna from the Torre degli Asinelli, erected in the first decades of the twelfth century,
and above, the drawing room of Palazzo Bosdari towards the small back garden*

The ceiling of Grazia Gazzoni's bedroom

named, actually originated a little farther along the Via Emilia, between the cities of Parma and Reggio in the Enza valley. The pasture of this district gives a unique quality to cow's milk and a kind of ecosystem has developed over the centuries among the area's three most important products. When the milk is skimmed to make cheese, the cream goes to produce superb butter, *burro di panna*; the whey left over is fed to the pigs that are being raised for prosciutto and the curd is aged to become the famous wheel of Parmesan.

One of the benedictions bestowed on the pilgrim traveling this route is the chance to taste both prosciutto and Parmesan cheese at their source. What a picnic can be put together along this stretch of the Via Emilia! When you try prosciutto here, do not have it sliced paper-thin. Instead, enjoy a hand-cut piece thick enough to chew, so you are able to relish its tender texture and sweet flavor. Here, too, you can taste Parmesan not only as a superior seasoning for another dish but as a cheese on its own. Bite into a freshly cut chunk. It will be pale gold in color, slightly crumbly in texture, a bit moist, aromatic, sharp and savory. Most of all, it will make you wonder if you have ever tasted the real thing before. At this point all that is lacking for a most memorable snack is bread and wine. The local bakery will have fresh *pasta dura* rolls with hard crusts and dense, cottony white insides, shaped in a variety of forms. Luckily we are in the heart of Lambrusco country so there is plenty of that pleasant, sparkling red at hand. And for dessert there are black cherries from nearby Vignola, sweet and hard, and Italy's best.

About midway along the Via Emilia there is another obligatory stop for the traveling gourmet, the charming city of Modena. On the popular plane of gastronomy it is famous for *zampone* and *cotechino*. The first is boned pig's foot stuffed with minced, spiced pork. It is simmered for several hours over low heat and served sliced and piping hot, often with other separately cooked boiled meats such as tongue,

miles from Piacenza on the border of Lombardia to Rimini on the Adriatic coast. It is a straight stretch of road that links together a chain of medieval cities whose very names evoke fine food.

In the spirit set by Artusi an epicurean pilgrimage would have to include a visit to Parma, synonymous in the English-speaking world with ham (even though Toscana and Umbria also produce a most excellent prosciutto, savory rather than sweet) and whose ancient Duchy gave its name to what is perhaps the best-known cheese in the world. Parmigiano Reggiano, as this cheese is officially chicken, ham, and beef. This traditional *bollito misto* is usually accompanied by boiled vegetables and mashed potatoes. *Cotechino* is made with the same stuffing as *zampone*, but in the form of a large salame, and lentils are its classical accompanying dish.

On a more elevated level of epicurean delights Modena kept its most precious culinary secret hidden for centuries in its attics, cellars and back rooms. Among outsiders, only the cognoscenti were aware of its existence. Today, even though its name and commercially produced substitutes have become popular, the genuine item is still rare and costly. This unique essence is called *aceto balsamico*, balsamic vinegar, although simply *balsamico* or balsam is more correct. This better suggests its medieval origins and medicinal, even alchemistical, purposes, for it was considered a soothing and healing balm before it was prized as a gastronomic condiment.

Unlike wine vinegar it is started with unfermented grape juice, the must from the pressing of mainly sweet Trebbiano grapes. This is boiled very slowly in copper pots until it is reduced to a sweet, thick syrup called *saba*. At this point a mother vinegar is mixed in and it is then poured into a wooden cask to ferment. This is the beginning of a complex, lengthy and costly process of ageing during which the *balsamico* is blended with older vintages and moved into a series of casks, all of different woods. Oak, chestnut, mulberry, juniper and cherry add their particular flavors and fragrance. What emerges after this decades-long journey is a gleaming, dark brown liquid, almost syrupy, with a complex, fragrant aroma that is penetrating and pleasingly acidic. It has a sweet-tart flavor that is quite intense.

In the area of Modena genuine *balsamico* is still made by several hundred families for their own private use. Only a few of them produce it to sell. In these cellars you can taste samples whose genealogies go back over a hundred years and are so mellow they can be drunk like a liqueur. I once attended a wedding feast at

Palazzo Bosdari's dining room set for a sumptuous feast

which we toasted the bride and groom not with cups of champagne but with thimbles of the families' ancient *balsamico* that boasted in its blend some of the grand duke's very own Riserva.

Balsamico's alchemistical properties are easily tested in the kitchen where it works delightful transformations. I often mix a few drops of the essence with my wine vinegar to dress salads. A tablespoonful added to risotto at the last minute of cooking adds a tasty tang. It also works extremely well in marinades for roast meats and an American friend of mine calls it his favorite steak sauce. Try using it to deglaze your sauté pan. For dessert it is excellent over strawberries and for the ultimate snack, sprinkle some over thin slices of the finest quality Parmesan cheese.

If we were to bypass Bologna for the

moment and continue along the Via Emilia, in less than an hour we would arrive at the sea in Rimini and be in another whole world of Emilia-Romagna cuisine. The Adriatic is Italy's prime source for quantity and variety of fish, so it is no wonder that its coastal towns have such an abundance of seafood specialties. In Ravenna, a few miles north of Rimini on the coastal road, one can sit down to a huge bowl of *brodetto*, soup made with a dozen different kinds of small fish. Farther up the coast eels are raised in the immense lagoon of Comacchio. Here you can eat them fresh out of the water, grilled, roasted or cooked with tomatoes. These *anguille* are also preserved *carpionate*, that is, first fried, then soaked in vinegar and finally flavored with garlic, bay and sage.

It would, however, be a sacrilege to bypass the gastronomic capital of Northern Italy and

Bologna's shops carry a wide variety of local cheeses

Artusi's "holy of holies" of Italian cuisine on an epicurean pilgrimage, so back we go to Bologna.

Whenever I visit Bologna it is the pasta that tempts me most. The Bolognesi have refined this culinary staple to an art. They make it by hand with superior flour and eggs and their skilled *sfogliatrici* roll it transparently thin. It comes in all sizes from tiny *tortellini* to large *tortelli*; in all shapes, from narrow ribbons of *tagliatelle* to broad sheets of *lasagne*. Usually it is filled, either stuffed, layered or served with such a thick meat sauce that it amounts to the same thing. Into their disk-shaped *tortellini* the Bolognesi stuff a fine paste of prosciutto, turkey, veal, egg, cheese and spices, especially nutmeg. In the Romagna part of the region this same pasta is cut into squares and formed into little peaked caps called *cappelletti*. The classic way to eat these is in broth, but they are also delicious in a butter and cream sauce. *Lasagne verdi*, green because of the finely shredded spinach added to the dough, is layered with butter, grated cheese, meat sauce, sometimes *besciamella*, and baked in the oven. For *tagliatelle* the classic Bolognese sauce is *ragù*, a thick stew of onions, carrots, pork, veal, butter, and tomatoes, often further enriched with dried mushrooms, chicken livers and cream.

Bologna did not become "fat" on pasta alone. What many connoisseurs consider the world's best sausage, mortadella, originated here, although ones not bought on the spot can be disappointing. If not the best, it can certainly be the biggest, when it is stuffed into the skin of an entire suckling pig. It is made from pure, finely chopped pork and highly seasoned, especially with peppercorns. Because of its smooth texture and subtle flavor, I find it an excellent seasoning for other dishes, meat rolls and loaves for example. The veal in Bologna is excellent and the city's cooks use it for one of their most opulent dishes, *costolette alla bolognese*, in which veal chops are prepared with three of the region's most delectable foods – Parmesan, prosciutto and white truffles. One of Bologna's most celebrated restaurants is famous for cooking turkey breasts in the same way.

Desserts tend toward rich and creamy city-style pastry. With your after-dinner coffee have a Majani chocolate, made in a small factory outside the city by the Majani family, which has owned and operated it since 1796. To help digest all of this, try a small glass of *nocino* liqueur made from green walnuts shelled, soaked in alcohol with lemon peel, cinnamon and cloves and aged in oak. According to tradition, the nuts must be picked at dawn on June 24, the feast of Saint John the Baptist, while they are still wet with dew. Only in Emilia-Romagna, it is said, could they have come up with the idea of making a liqueur from nuts. I like its slightly bitter aftertaste that cuts the sweetness. It is reputed to have impressive "medicinal" qualities as well as being a good *digestivo* – and it is superb as a topping for ice cream, should anyone still be hungry!

I would not want all this talk about food and eating to give the impression that Bologna is only a city of gourmets and gourmands. In many ways it also happens to be one of the most handsome and livable cities in Italy. Over the centuries it has taken shape much like a cartwheel. At the hub are its two medieval landmark towers, leaning at remarkable angles and somewhat ungainly but with the lovely names of Asinelli and Garisenda. The outside rim is formed by the ancient city walls and gates and connecting them to the center are literally miles of colonnaded streets lined with magnificent churches and palaces, all painted in various tones of apricot and Pompeian red. Also in the center is the splendid Piazza Maggiore with the immense Basilica di San Petronio and the monumental Neptune fountain by the Renaissance sculptor, Giambologna.

The Bolognesi themselves are a cheerful, friendly people, not corrupted or jaded by international tourism. Bologna, in fact, has remained a very Italian city. Its citizens possess an enlightened civic sense and enjoy a stimulating cultural life. Both their national gallery, *La Pinacoteca Nazionale*, and opera house, *Il Teatro*

Atti confectionery, renowned throughout the region

Piazza Maggiore, Bologna

Comunale, produce artistic events of international importance. Its university has exercized a centuries-long civilizing effect on the city – the University of Bologna is the oldest in the Western world and recently celebrated its nine-hundredth anniversary – and is still a prestigious and vital institution of higher learning.

While my daughter, Emanuela, was attending the University of Bologna she lived with our friends, Giuseppe and Grazia Gazzoni,

whom my husband and I have known for thirty years. Giuseppe is from an ancient Bolognese family and owns and manages one of the city's oldest industries, founded by his family at the beginning of the century. Grazia is a Florentine who somewhat reluctantly left her city when she married Giuseppe, only to discover that Bologna proved to be an ideal place to live. It has provided a sane environment for raising her son and two daughters as well as a conducive atmosphere for pursuing her own

intellectual and cultural interests, especially the study of art and medieval history. She is a dynamic yet private person who enjoys nothing more than gathering together in her gracious and comfortable home a small and intimate group of persons for a meal at which a genuine exchange of ideas and experience can take place. Bologna also furnishes ample opportunities for this kind of social life. As a guest of the Gazzoni it is not unusual to find yourself in the company of the rector of the university or the

Bologna is famous for its arcaded streets

director of the opera house together with prestigious visitors and performing artists who have been drawn to Bologna by these two poles of its cultural life.

At Grazia's table a felicitous meeting takes place between *Bologna la Grassa* and *la Dotta*, the Learned, each keeping the other from taking itself too seriously. She also keeps her menus in balance. They are intended to stimulate conversation, not bring on somnolence. Her recipes draw on the richness of traditional Bolognese cuisine, yet are not so heavy as to dull the mind. I remember one dish that made an internationally celebrated soprano trill with delight. It consisted of a very large *raviolo* filled with a whole egg yolk that ran golden when she cut into it. And the creamy lemon sauce on the tender, young asparagus from Ravenna that accompanied the veal cutlets sautéed with herbs would soothe even the most overtaxed vocal cords. A traditional yet unusual Emilia-Romagna combination that made an award-winning author lick his bearded chops was cotechino sausage topped with a warm zabaglione sauce – very rich, but followed by a light, refreshing dessert of strawberries in balsamic vinegar. Giuseppe is also president of the

Bologna Italian Manufacturers' Association and for his colleagues in industry Grazia often prepares the area's superior veal roasted to exquisite tenderness, preceded by gnocchi in a sauce of Parmesan cheese. There is a pause even in the most animated discussion when *torta di capelli d'angelo* is served for dessert. It is a fresh ricotta tart with almonds and candied fruit, baked in a pastry of angel-hair pasta.

Grazia chooses the wines that accompany her meals with great care. For white she favors the dry, fruity Pinots from the hillside vineyards surrounding Bologna. Her preferred red is the region's unique Barbarossa and with desserts, Vin Santo from Romagna. Her essential criterion is that they be *genuino*. She would want neither the evening's drink nor the conversation to give a headache to her guests.

Only fifty miles over the Apennine mountains from Bologna lies Toscana, where I spend much of my time. For many Northerners this is the boundary between Northern and Southern Italy, although Tuscans certainly do not consider themselves "Southerners" but rather a race apart – superior, of course, to both. Yet, gastronomically at least, there can be no question that once over the Apennines one has left Northern Italy. In the fields, sheep take the place of cattle (with the notable exception of the Val di Chiana in Toscana where the beef for a genuine *bistecca alla fiorentina* is raised) and rice has been left well behind. Olive oil replaces butter in the kitchen and *pasta secca*, dry pasta of the macaroni variety, will be brought to the table far more frequently than *pasta all'uovo* of the tagliatelle type. The regions of Northern Italy have their special dishes with garlic, e.g. *bagna cauda* in Piemonte and *pesto* in Liguria, but now *aglio* will appear as an essential ingredient in practically every dish. It therefore always strikes me as highly appropriate that when traveling by *autostrada* from Bologna to Firenze the first rest stop on the Tuscan side is named "Aglio."

Poplar plantations in the Po Delta echo the arcades of the Emilian plain

MENU FOR A DIVA

RAVIOLI ALLE UOVA
Egg ravioli

COSTOLETTE ALLE ERBE
Veal chops with herbs

ASPARAGI IN SALSA DI LIMONE
Asparagus with lemon sauce

PERE AI MIRTILLI
Stewed pears with blueberries

These ravioli are a specialty of this region's justly celebrated restaurant, San Domenico in Imola, which continues the culinary tradition of the old Italian families. I think this would be the consummate dish for a brunch. While boiling, some ravioli may float to the top of the water (because air has remained inside the pocket of pasta.) In that case, hold them under with a slotted spoon.

The aromatic recipe for the cutlets also works well with butterflied chicken breasts. The lemon sauce for the asparagus is a light version of a hollandaise, more suited to the taste of our times than that heavier sauce served so frequently in the *cucina alto-borghese*. Raspberries instead of blueberries are also delicious with the pears.

Suggested Wines For all three menus try the recommendations of Grazia Gazzoni; they are among the region's finest. For whites, the Pinot Bianco and Pinot Grigio made by Enrico Vallania in the Colli Bolognesi, dry, scented and fruity; for a unique red, an aged Barbarossa di Bertinoro by Mario Pezzi, full-bodied and opulent; with dessert, the Vin Santo di Montericco of the Conti Pasolini Dall' Onda.

RAVIOLI ALLE UOVA
Egg ravioli

7 oz/scant 1½ cups/200 g plain (all-purpose) flour
2 eggs
8 oz/1 cup/225 g ricotta cheese
3½ oz/scant 1 cup/100 g grated Parmesan cheese
4 tbsp chopped parsley
6 egg yolks
3½ oz/7 tbsp/100 g butter
1 handful fresh sage leaves
salt and pepper

Make a dough for homemade pasta with flour and eggs (as explained on page 188), working until smooth and elastic. Pat into 2 flat rectangles to fit the size of the pasta machine and roll them to obtain 2 very thin sheets, approximately 4 in/10 cm wide.

Make the filling by combining ricotta, half the Parmesan and the parsley. Season with salt and pepper. Along 1 sheet of dough, shape 6 mounds of filling into 'nests' spaced 4 in/10 cm apart and place a whole egg yolk in the center of each. Cover with the second sheet, making sure that no air is trapped inside. Seal and divide the ravioli using a round pastry cutter.

Melt butter with sage over moderate heat. Bring a large saucepan of salted water to a boil, cook the ravioli for 2 minutes. When they rise to the surface remove with a slotted spoon and drain. Place 1 on each dish, sprinkle with the remaining cheese, pour over the sage-butter mixture and serve.

COSTOLETTE ALLE ERBE
Veal chops with herbs

2 eggs
salt
6 tbsp chopped rosemary, oregano, thyme, sage
7 oz/1¾ cups/200 g fine dry breadcrumbs
6 veal chops
3½ oz/7 tbsp/100 g butter
1 lemon

Beat the eggs with a little salt. Mix the chopped herbs together and then mix with the breadcrumbs. Dip the chops in the egg and coat with the herbed breadcrumbs.

Heat the butter in a frying pan and cook the chops until golden brown on both sides. Place on a serving dish, surround with lemon wedges and serve.

ASPARAGI IN SALSA DI LIMONE
Asparagus with lemon sauce

4½ lb/2 kg asparagus
For the sauce:
2 oz/4 tbsp/50 g butter
2 tbsp plain (all-purpose) flour
18 fl oz/2¼ cups/500 ml chicken broth at room temperature (page 189)
1 egg yolk
4 fl oz/½ cup/125 ml whipping cream
juice of 1 lemon
salt

To cook the asparagus, tie in a bundle and boil in a deep pan of salted water with the tips up. Drain, remove string, arrange on a platter and keep warm until the sauce is ready.

While the asparagus is cooking, make the sauce. Heat half the butter in a saucepan, add

the flour and cook over low heat until completely blended. Add the broth, a little at a time, mixing well. Remove from the heat, add the egg yolk, mixing continuously with a whisk. Put the sauce over low heat in a double boiler, adding the remaining butter a little at a time, whisking continually.

Remove the sauce from the heat, add the cream, lemon juice and salt and pour over the asparagus immediately before serving.

PERE AI MIRTILLI
Stewed pears with blueberries

6 pears, suitable for cooking
18 fl oz/2¼ cups/500 ml red wine
5 oz/⅔ cup/150 g sugar
grated peel of ½ lemon
7 oz/2 cups/200 g blueberries

Peel the pears, leaving on any stems. Place in a casserole together with the wine, sugar and lemon peel. Cover and cook over low heat for about 10 minutes. Remove pears from the syrup and set on serving plates.

Pass the berries through a food mill. Reduce the syrup by three-quarters, remove from the heat and stir in the puréed berries. Pour the sauce over the pears, leave to cool and serve.

Ravioli alle uova

Asparagi in salsa di limone
Sfogliata di cappelletti

MENU FOR AN AWARD-WINNING AUTHOR

SFOGLIATA DI CAPPELLETTI
Cappelletti pie

COTECHINO·ALLO ZABAIONE
Cotechino sausage with zabaglione sauce

ZUCCHINE RIPIENE
Stuffed courgettes (zucchini)

FRAGOLE ALL'ACETO BALSAMICO
Strawberries in balsamic vinegar

When pressed for time, I use frozen pastry. There are also several good brands of dried cappelletti generally available to speed preparation of this pie.

Cotechino with zabaglione sauce and lentils is a classic dish for the family celebration of New Year's Eve, washed down with lots of spumante, of course. Lentils symbolize money, which equals prosperity. With or without the lentils, it is a different and delicious dish for any supper party.

Balsamic vinegar, or a fine-quality red wine vinegar, works wonders when your strawberries are not quite so flavorful.

SFOGLIATA DI CAPPELLETTI
Cappelletti pie

14 oz/400 g puff pastry (page 188)
7 oz/scant 1½ cups/200 g plain (all-purpose) flour and 2 large eggs for pasta dough
For the filling:
3 oz/100 g mortadella sausage
3 oz/100 g ham
2 oz/50 g sweet Italian sausage
2 tbsp dried pórcini mushrooms, soaked in water for 30 minutes and squeezed dry
1 tsp juniper berries
1 tbsp fine dry breadcrumbs
1 egg
pinch of grated nutmeg
3½ oz/scant 1 cup/100 g grated Parmesan cheese
salt and pepper
To serve:
2 oz/4 tbsp/50 g butter
4 fl oz/½ cup/125 ml whipping cream

To make the filling, finely mince or grind together the mortadella, ham, sausage, mushrooms and juniper berries. Add the breadcrumbs, egg, nutmeg, and 2 tbsp of the Parmesan. Add salt and pepper to taste. Mix together well and refrigerate.

Roll out the pastry and use to line a 9 in/23 cm French flan (tart) pan with a removable base, that has been buttered and lightly floured. Cover the dough with parchment (silicon) paper, fill with dried beans and cook in a preheated oven at 350°F/180°C/Mark 4 for about 20 minutes. Remove beans and paper and cook for another 20 minutes.

Prepare the pasta dough (page 188.) Using a pasta machine, roll it out as thinly as possible into long strips 2 in/5 cm wide.

Place about half a teaspoon of filling in little mounds along one half of the width of the strip at a distance of about 1 in/2.5 cm apart. Fold over the uncovered half and seal each mound firmly by pressing down with the fingers. Cut the strip into 1 in/2.5 cm squares. Bend the lower corners around the finger to form the shape of little hats, *cappelletti.*

While the puff pastry is baking, heat the butter and cream and cook the cappelletti in a saucepan of salted boiling water for a couple of minutes. Drain, season with the butter and cream. Pour into the puff pastry case, sprinkle with the remaining Parmesan and serve.

COTECHINO ALLO ZABAIONE
Cotechino sausage with zabaglione sauce

1 cotechino sausage (about 1¾ lb/800g)
2 egg yolks
3 tbsp sugar
4 tbsp Marsala

Make a few incisions with a needle in the skin of the cotechino. Wrap in muslin (cheesecloth) and tie, then place in a long, narrow flameproof casserole or large saucepan and cover completely with cold water. Simmer slowly for about 2½ hours. Drain and set aside for a few minutes.

Meanwhile, beat the egg yolks and the sugar with a wire whisk until creamy. Place in a double boiler, add Marsala and continue to whip until the zabaglione thickens.

When the cotechino is drained, remove the cloth and arrange in slices on a serving platter. Pour the hot zabaglione around and serve.

ZUCCHINE RIPIENE
Stuffed courgettes (zucchini)

6 medium courgettes (zucchini)
3½ oz/⅓ cup/100 g ricotta
1 egg, separated
2 oz/1 cup/50 g chopped parsley
2 oz/½ cup/50 g grated Parmesan cheese
1 oz/2 tbsp/25 g butter
salt and pepper

Boil the courgettes (zucchini) in salted water for a few minutes. Cut off a thin strip from one side. Scrape out about half the insides and discard.

Mix the ricotta, egg yolk, parsley, Parmesan cheese, salt and pepper. Beat the egg white to stiff peaks and fold into the stuffing mixture. Using a piping (pastry) bag, fill the courgettes (zucchini) generously.

Arrange the vegetables in a buttered baking dish and dot their tops with butter. Bake in a preheated oven at 350°F/180°C/Mark 4 for 40 minutes, or until the insides are firm and the top of the filling is golden brown. Keep moist by adding a few tablespoons of water to the baking dish when necessary.

Cotechino allo zabaione

FRAGOLE ALL'ACETO BALSAMICO
Strawberries in balsamic vinegar

1 lb/3 cups/450 g strawberries

3 tbsp balsamic vinegar

3 tbsp sugar

Clean and halve or quarter the strawberries into serving bowls. Sprinkle on the vinegar, then the sugar. Refrigerate for 2 hours before serving. Top each serving with whipped cream if desired.

87

The gnocchi can be made well ahead of time, refrigerated in their dish and baked at the last minute. Try Gorgonzola melted with cream as a tasty variation of the cheese, or a bechamel with *funghi porcini* (dried mushrooms.)

While cooking the veal for the four hours, it is essential not to lose faith. It will not dry out and, moreover, it will emerge a miracle of tenderness. Keep it uncovered and if it has still not browned sufficiently near the end, turn up the heat to 400°F/200°C/Mark 6 for the last 20 minutes.

The pasta tart must be eaten while still hot. Fresh taglierini also bake into a good pastry crust.

GNOCCHI FONDENTI
Gnocchi with Parmesan cheese

8 fl oz/1 cup/225 ml milk
pinch of salt
6 oz/12 tbsp/180 g butter
10 oz/2 cups/300 g plain (all purpose) flour
4 eggs
grated nutmeg
8 oz/2 cups/225 g grated Parmesan cheese
8 fl oz/1 cup/225 ml whipping cream

Heat the milk to a boil with salt and butter. Remove from the heat and add the flour, stirring continuously. Return to the heat and cook until the dough comes together. Cool for a few minutes, then add the eggs one by one, beating until air bubbles begin to form. Add the nutmeg and ¾ of the Parmesan.

Put the dough into a piping (pastry) bag with a large tip. Squeeze gnocchi out into a pan of boiling salted water, cutting off cylinders with the blade of a knife. Allow the gnocchi to cook for a couple of minutes after they have risen to the surface. Remove with a slotted spoon and put in an ovenproof dish.

Heat the cream with the remaining Parmesan over low heat and pour over the gnocchi. Bake for 20 minutes at 400°F/200°C/Mark 6 until golden.

STINCO AL LIMONE
Veal shank with lemon sauce

1 shin of veal (veal shank), about 3 lb/1.5 kg
3 sprigs rosemary, finely chopped
salt and pepper
1 tbsp plain (all-purpose) flour
2 oz/4 tbsp/50 g butter
1 glass white wine
2 egg yolks
2 tbsp lemon juice
grated peel of 1 lemon
2 tbsp chopped parsley
8 fl oz/1 cup/225 ml meat broth (page 189)

Slit the veal lengthwise to the bone in several places. Stuff with rosemary mixed with a little salt. Tie the shank top to bottom with a string. Season with salt and pepper.

Flour the veal on all sides. Put in a flame-proof casserole with the butter and cook in the oven at 300°F/150°C/Mark 2 for 4 hours.

Remove the meat, pour off the fat, and deglaze the casserole with white wine. In a bowl, beat the egg yolks together with the lemon juice, lemon peel, chopped parsley and broth. Pour the mixture into the casserole and over very low heat let this sauce thicken very slightly for about 1 minute. Slice the meat and arrange on a platter, pour over the sauce and serve.

INSALATA AL BALSAMICO
Salad with balsamic vinegar

1 head Boston or similar lettuce
1 handful parsley leaves
1 handful rocket (arugula)
1 handful escarole or curly endive
little dill, mint leaves, summer savory
2 slices prosciutto, cut very thinly
1 oz/2 tbsp/25 g butter
salt and pepper
1 tbsp red wine vinegar
1 tbsp balsamic vinegar
5 tbsp extra virgin olive oil

Mix the lettuces and leaves in a bowl. Cut the prosciutto into strips and sauté with the butter in a heavy frying pan. Dissolve salt with wine vinegar, add pepper, balsamic vinegar and olive oil and mix well. Pour mixture on the salad, toss well and serve.

TORTA DI CAPELLI D'ANGELO
Angel-hair tart

8 oz/1 cup/225 g ricotta
3 eggs, separated
3½ oz/generous ⅓ cup/100 g sugar
grated peel of 1 orange
3½ oz/½ cup/100 g candied fruit, cut into pieces
3½ oz/⅔ cup/100 g almonds, toasted and chopped
7 oz/200 g angel-hair pasta
salt

Sieve the ricotta, add the egg yolks, sugar, orange peel, candied fruit and half the almonds. Mix well.

Cook the pasta for 2 minutes in a pan of

Torta di capelli d'angelo

lightly salted boiling water. Drain and combine with the ricotta mixture.

Beat the egg whites into stiff peaks and gently add to the mixture. Butter a spring-clip (springform) pan and sprinkle with the remaining almonds. Pour in the mixture and cook in a preheated oven at 180°F/350°C/Mark 4 for about 1 hour. Remove from the pan and serve immediately.

TOSCANA

BADIA A COLTIBUONO IN CHIANTI

*Family-style entertaining in an eleventh-century abbey, home
of Lorenza de'Medici and Piero Stucchi-Prinetti*

I live in an eleventh-century castle which for the first eight hundred years of its existence was a fortified Benedictine abbey and for the last almost two hundred years the hereditary home of my husband's family, the Giuntini. Great-grandfather Guido Giuntini, who was a Florentine banker, purchased Badia a Coltibuono after Napoleon had confiscated the property from the monks. Since then the estate has been managed by the family and used as a

country residence. Today it is practically our year-round home.

I still remember vividly the first time I saw Coltibuono. In those days the drive from Milano was long and exhausting and this was a particularly sweltering August day. Finally, about midway between Firenze and Siena, we began to climb into the Chianti hills through a landscape of vineyards and olive groves until we reached an altitude of over two thousand

*Early morning panorama across Chianti and the Elsa valley
and above, Badia a Coltibuono seen from the garden*

91

feet and there it was: magnificent and majestic, austere but not harsh, its cut-stone buildings reflecting a rose hue in the late afternoon sun and its medieval campanile dominating the over two thousand acres of surrounding primeval forests.

The residential part of the abbey, which has been lived in for almost a millennium, is full of history. Its architectural adaptation down through the centuries tells a fascinating story, in particular with regard to its culinary past and present. For example, what is now our family room was originally the medieval kitchen of the abbey. Today it houses all the electronic trappings usual in a room where four children have grown up – stereo, TV and video. Nonetheless, it still proudly possesses its splendid open hearth where Brother Cook prepared his monastic meals and where in winter our family – my youngest son, Guido, especially – love to hold barbecues *alla toscana*, usually consisting of a mixed grill of *bistecca alla fiorentina*, fresh pork sausages made by our village butcher, Vincenzo, and *rostinciana*, succulent Tuscan spareribs. I sometimes feel these carnivorous family feasts are held in periodic revolt against what is considered my unfair weighting of menus in favor of greens, pasta and the lighter white meats.

Hanging on the wall opposite the fireplace is a life-size sixteenth-century portrait of an ancestor of mine, Alessandro de'Medici, who became Pope Leo XI. I do not think His Holiness would approve of everything that goes on around him these days, yet he himself lost the papacy after only two weeks when he died of gluttony! Anyhow, I have always taken his presence in this room, which preceded mine, as an omen, portending good, I hope. It seems my family was destined to have a long history of involvement with Coltibuono.

Giovanni de'Medici, son of Lorenzo the Magnificent, held the abbey as a lucrative fiefdom for a brief period in the late fifteenth century, as did his cousin, Giuliano de'Medici after him. Francesca, the granddaughter of

Lorenzo, married another de'Medici and went to live in Ottaviano, near Napoli, where they founded my branch of the family. I like to imagine that this relative of mine visited her uncle's abbey. As a most prestigious visitor she would have eaten in the same splendid room where I now serve dinner to my guests.

Whether Il Magnifico himself ever visited Coltibuono, no one knows. What can be presumed with a certain amount of certainty is that he drank its wine and sampled some of the game from its forest. It just so happened that the Abbot of Coltibuono was the brother of one of the most influential persons in the Medici court, the humanist philosopher and poet, Baccio Ugolini. During a summer holiday at Badia he sent a letter to Lorenzo, accompanied with some wine, in an attempt to convince him to visit. The letter, preserved in the archives, reads in part: "... the red wine here is much better than at Vallombrosa [another Tuscan abbey Lorenzo used to visit] and the white is as good if not better. The hot weather brings on a good thirst and there is the cooling shade of pine trees and murmuring streams." An amusing and intentionally equivocal reference to frolicking in the woods with some nymphs follows.

His brother, the Abbot, seems to have enjoyed another kind of hunting the surrounding forest provides. He sent Lorenzo a wild boar that he had shot on an expedition, with a letter explaining that it was the only one that did not get away. It is somehow reassuring to think that today we are still enjoying meals of wild boar with red wine from Coltibuono. The boar is usually downed by our gardener, Virgilio, who is an avid huntsman, and I prepare it in the traditional Tuscan way, with a sweet and savory sauce of red wine vinegar and chocolate. Rumor has it that even the occasional nymph has been spotted in the forest!

Back to the culinary history the architectural adaptation of the house tells. The progression, or regression might be more exact, of the dining rooms down through the centuries is

particularly interesting from this point of view. The monks' Renaissance refectory is now our drawing room, which we use for large receptions. It is a grand, frescoed room with cornices and vaulted ceiling. I have furnished it simply, with large white sofas and armchairs, and one can still get a feeling, I think, of its monastic past. Next to the refectory was the monastery's guest dining room, which I use on more formal occasions. It, too, is fifteenth century, but was redecorated in the eighteenth century with splendid baroque stuccos, the work of visiting monks from Germany, perhaps in exchange for their room and board. Through this room one arrives at the former kitchen, now our family room. Off of this are two rooms that used to be pantries and service space and are today our family dining room and kitchen, most recently remodeled to accommodate my cooking classes.

Looking back through this passage of rooms as well as of time, almost a thousand years, one can see that as household help diminished (the monks had their lay brothers to look after the kitchen and serve at meals and my mother-in-law had a staff of seven, whereas I have one daily and occasional outside help) the dining room and kitchen moved nearer to each other and both diminished in size, although they are still relatively large rooms by today's standards. This translocation and adaptation of kitchen and dining space tell a parallel story about the evolution of cooking and entertaining at Coltibuono.

In the days when my mother-in-law, Maria Luisa Giuntini, was mistress of the house, there was only one place where meals were taken, the formal dining room, and everyone dressed for the occasion, including the servants! Children, of course, were to be seen and not heard. As mine were growing up, they were usually relegated to their own miniature dining room. After meals, family and friends would retire to the ancient refectory hall to play music, billiards and more often, cards. Marilù, as Maria Luisa was called, had gathered around

The drawing room of Badia

her something of a salon that included such personalities as Nicky Mariano, Bernard Berenson, Giulietta Mendelssohn, Gaspar Cassadò and John Pope Hennessy. I wonder what they, not to mention the monks, would think if they could observe some of the after-dinner gatherings that have taken place here in more recent times. I think of parties like the one we had at the conclusion of the very first week of cooking classes at Coltibuono, when a group of lively Southern Californians (and myself) danced to the likes of Madonna and the Pointer Sisters.

Coltibuono has so many facets – medieval abbey, modern winery and farm, major Tuscan cultural and scenic attraction – that on initial impact it can be rather overwhelming. When the household became mine to manage, however, I decided that above all it was our family home and no matter what kind of entertaining the occasion might require, it ought always to fit into and be an expression of our family life. The times when the entire family is able to sit down and share a meal together are rare and I was not about to banish my children and their friends from the table

because there was "official" entertaining on the agenda. We continuously have guests from the international world of wine, art and politics and as it turns out, I think they are happily surprised and pleased to experience family hospitality within the walls of this sometimes formidable medieval monastery.

Also, Coltibuono is our country home. For many years, while the children were growing up and my husband's work as well as my own centered in Milano, it was where we spent all our leisure time, long weekends, holidays and the summer months. It is where we relax with

The new glassed-in cloisters of Badia

family and friends. I swim, garden, take long hikes through the splendid Chianti countryside, visit our interesting neighbors who have settled in Toscana from all over Italy – indeed, from all over the world.

These personal circumstances have set the tone for entertaining and eating at Coltibuono. A family, and therefore informal, atmosphere prevails. We give a fair share of more formal dinner parties, too, but I hope that even on these occasions the pervading mood is relaxed and familiar. I must confess that it was only recently I began to use on occasion "proper" wine glasses at the table. I had safely stored away Marilù's footed Bohemian crystal and I did not hesitate to serve even fine old vintages of Coltibuono in our simple, everyday glassware. Some of our American guests went away thinking it was "radical chic." I think British visitors, especially from the wine trade, were slightly scandalized and God knows what the French thought! For me it was, I suppose, a sort of unconscious symbol of the family style of hospitality I wanted to extend.

In the same spirit, I have always tried to compose menus with dishes that can be prepared beforehand, or at least ones that can be cooked with a minimum of last-minute fuss and bother and still not lose their freshness. These days one cannot always count on the luxury of help in the kitchen. Besides, I enjoy cooking for guests myself. Yet I also want to be able to enjoy their company both before and during the meal. I do not want to spend the evening in the kitchen. Therefore, I tend toward simple, uncomplicated recipes.

On the other hand, there is a culinary heritage to uphold at Coltibuono. The dining table of a Tuscan *fattoria* (wine-farm) is traditionally a place where guests have come to expect the finest food and hospitality. Fine wine and olive oil, the farm's two principal products, have a strong affinity for fine food. Living and entertaining in a place as grand and gracious as the Badia imposes, as well as elicits, a certain style and elegance. Coltibuono has also become the center for my cooking classes and I certainly believe in putting to practice what I preach. Fortunately, we live in Toscana where the civilization as well as the regional

gastronomic tradition provides all the necessary ingredients, both cultural and culinary, in order to combine simplicity and elegance.

Toscana is a land of unparalleled natural and man-made beauty and unique among the twenty-three regions of Italy in its combination of a landscape both wild and cultivated, natural and civilized, yet all held together in harmony. The entire culture of Toscana, it seems to me, is determined by a fine balance of tastes, and that certainly holds true for its cuisine.

Toscana is also the region where the cooking has been least affected by outside influences. Even the *cucina alto-borghese toscana* remained essentially regional. In fact, it was Tuscan regional cooking that influenced other cuisines. They say it was Caterina de'Medici who introduced to France *canard à l'orange* or, as she would have said, *anitra all'arancia*, along with other such civilizing Italian culinary traditions as the use of the fork and spoon.

It has often been said that there is really no classic Italian cuisine, meaning that Italian cooking is essentially regional in character. I would argue, from the past as well as the present, that just as Toscana is the most typical of Italian places, so is Tuscan cooking the most Italian of cuisines. It is certainly the Italian culinary tradition that has most influenced the talented young American chefs of today.

Tuscan dishes are uncomplicated, vivid, fresh, earthy and wholesome. This is true of the *cucina alto-borghese* tradition as well as the *cucina povera*. Excellence depends on perfect ingredients, simply but knowingly prepared. Great attention is paid to raw materials, which must be of the highest quality, cooked with a minimum of sauces and seasoning. This does not mean, however, they are not refined or without elegance. On the contrary, they are almost ingeniously simple and effective.

A good example of this, and a favorite Tuscan winter dish, is roast loin of pork, stuffed with sage, rosemary and bay and served with a fennel sauce. Of course, the loin of pork must be the best. In fact, the dish is called *arista*, the name given to it, they say, by a Greek visitor to these parts who exclaimed upon tasting it, "arista," meaning in his language, "the best." This succulent piece of meat must then be seasoned judiciously so that its natural flavor stands out. The fennel sauce has a striking effect on this tender and aromatic dish. It is light, fresh and very tasty. *Arista* makes a simple and delicious second course and an elegant one, when served on the bone with the fennel sauce at the side.

Another harmonious aspect of Tuscan civilization and cuisine is the natural link between culture and countryside, even between city and country. Tuscans like their food fresh from the land. They seem to be born good gardeners and are, for better or worse, avid hunters. Marilu lived about six months of the year at Coltibuono and the other six months in Firenze. When she was in the city, however, an almost daily cartload of farm produce was sent to her from Coltibuono. In just such ways Tuscan *cucina alto-borghese* literally kept in contact with its roots. *Haute cuisine* that has evolved in the city often loses its earthy flavor and has to compensate accordingly.

A simple Tuscan dish, but one that has done many a Tuscan proud, is *spiedini di salsicce e fegatelli*, skewers of pork liver wrapped in caul net, special sweet Chianti sausage and small slices of country bread. It is difficult to tell which is the more delicious, the liver, sausage or the bread. I serve it with freshly shelled peas from the garden cooked with a bit of tarragon.

Another benefit of a cuisine still connected to the country is that menus are seasonal, whatever the land yields at the moment. This means that there is always something to look forward to. I think of game in the autumn, wild boar and pigeon (squab) and lots of mushrooms, especially the delicious porcini that grow in the woods surrounding Coltibuono and the marvelous white truffles that are now being extracted from the area around Siena. In the winter there are soups made of beans and flavored with our freshly pressed olive oil. In spring, greens galore and fresh sheep cheese and an abundance of fruit and vegetables all summer long.

There is a story that sums up much of what I would like to say about cooking and entertaining at Coltibuono. A couple of years ago a well-known personality from the world of "travel adventures" arrived unannounced at Coltibuono. He wanted to see what the place was like and whether it would be possible to arrange a series of visits for select clients. He rang the entrance bell and as he was dressed quite formally for the occasion, in dark jacket and tie, the housekeeper mistook him for the chauffeur of a group of New York cooking professionals whom I was entertaining that day at luncheon. She brought him straight to the kitchen, sat him down at the table and poured him a glass of wine. Then she spread out a damask cloth on the marble kitchen table and laid a place setting of silver and china. Before he could say anything, she was dishing up a plate of *risotto ai funghi porcini* that just happened to be ready. By this time he had heard talking and laughing coming from the adjoining dining-room and gathered that there had been some misunderstanding, but as he did not speak Italian and the housekeeper could not understand English, he was unable to clarify the situation. So he excused himself as best he could and departed, reluctantly leaving behind the risotto as well as the stuffed pigeon (squab) he had just glimpsed as it was coming out of the oven.

Only several months afterward, when finally we met, did he tell me that he went away from my kitchen feeling a little perplexed but thinking what marvelous hospitality – spontaneous, friendly, most informal yet elegant, and the food at least looked and smelled delicious. I would like this to be everyone's first and lasting impression of hospitality at Coltibuono, with the difference, of course, that my guests also get to taste their meal!

The alabaster abbey church of St Antimo, near Montalcino

MENU FOR A FAMILY SUPPER

MINESTRA DI FAGIOLI E LATTUGA
Bean and lettuce soup

ARISTA DI MAIALE AL FINOCCHIO
Roast pork with fennel

PATATE ALL'ALLORO
Potatoes with bay leaves

CROSTATA DI PERE AL CIOCCOLATO
Chocolate pear tart

This is an uncomplicated menu, permeated with the fragrance of the Chianti countryside and especially comforting on a cold winter's night. The soup is a lighter version of the traditional Tuscan peasant dish, *pasta e fagioli*. Its secret is in the seasoning and well made it does honor to the most elegant table. Chick peas may be substituted for the cannellini beans. It makes a nourishing light luncheon by itself, poured over a thick piece of toasted Italian bread doused with yet more olive oil.

The pork must be cooked slowly so all the fat melts and the meat becomes tender and golden brown. Be sure the fennel sauce has the consistency of a refined sauce and not a purée. For added aroma (not necessary with this savory roast) a half slice of bacon can be wrapped around each potato before putting in the oven.

You can dress up the tart for a more formal occasion with little rosettes of whipped cream.

Suggested Wines A fresh, young red with character will take you all the way through this meal, including the chocolate tart. I would serve the current vintage of Coltibuono Rosso, made from a blend of sangioveto and canaiolo nero and a touch of Tuscan Cabernet.

MINESTRA DI FAGIOLI E LATTUGA
Bean and lettuce soup

10 oz/1½ cups/300 g cannellini beans
2 oz/50 g pancetta
3 sprigs rosemary
2 garlic cloves
1 small onion
6 sprigs thyme
7 tbsp extra virgin olive oil
70 fl oz/8¾ cups/2 liters light meat broth
3 lettuce hearts
2 oz/4 tbsp/50 g butter
6 oz/180 g dried tagliatelle
salt and pepper

Soak the beans overnight in cold water, then drain. Chop the pancetta finely with 2 sprigs of the rosemary, the garlic, onion and thyme. Cook with 3 tablespoons of the olive oil for a few minutes over low heat until transparent. Pour the drained beans into the pan with the last sprig of rosemary. Add the broth, and simmer for about 1½ hours.

Pass half the beans through a food mill, and pour back into the soup. Blanch the lettuce hearts briefly in boiling water, and drain. Quarter the lettuce hearts, and braise in a covered saucepan with the butter.

Sauté ⅓ of the tagliatelle noodles in the remaining olive oil (they will break). Add them to the soup with the remaining tagliatelle, the lettuce hearts, a little salt and pepper and cook for a few minutes until the pasta is *al dente*. Serve immediately.

ARISTA DI MAIALE AL FINOCCHIO
Roast pork with fennel

1 sprig rosemary
4 cloves garlic
salt and pepper
2½ tsp fennel seeds
3 lb/1.2 kg pork loin, bones split

Arista di maiale al finocchio

2 oz/4 tbsp/50 g butter
1 tbsp extra virgin olive oil
1 fennel bulb
4 fl oz/¹⁄₂ cup/125 ml milk
8 fl oz/1 cup/225 ml white wine

Finely chop the rosemary and garlic. Add salt, pepper and the fennel seeds. Stuff this mixture into the cuts in the pork where the bones were split. Place the meat in a roasting pan with 1 oz/2 tbsp/25 g of the butter, and the olive oil, and cook in the oven at 325°F/170°C/Mark 3 for about 2 hours.

Roughly chop the fennel, then cook in a covered casserole with the remaining butter and a little water over low heat until tender.

Transfer to a blender, add the milk and blend until smooth.

When the meat is cooked, slice and arrange on a serving platter. Keep warm. Pour off the fat from the roasting pan, and deglaze with white wine. Boil for a couple of minutes, then add the fennel mixture, mix well and strain over the meat. Additional fennel sauce can be served at the table.

PATATE ALL'ALLORO
Potatoes with bay leaves

12 small potatoes, unpeeled
12 fresh bay leaves

4 tbsp extra virgin olive oil
salt and pepper

Preheat the oven to 350°F/180°C/Mark 4. Wash and dry the potatoes and make a lengthwise slit in each one. Put a bay leaf in the slit and season with salt and pepper. Heat the olive oil in a roasting pan on top of the stove. Set the potatoes side by side in the pan. Transfer to the oven and cook for about 1 hour, or until the potatoes are golden brown and easily pierced. Arrange around the roast pork and serve.

CROSTATA DI PERE AL CIOCCOLATO
Chocolate pear tart

4 oz/8 tbsp/125 g butter
7 oz/scant 1¹⁄₂ cups/200 g flour
1 egg
4 oz/¹⁄₂ cup/125 g sugar
2 oz/¹⁄₂ cup/50 g cocoa powder
2 oz/2 tbsp/50 g orange marmalade
2 pears
Chocolate filling:
3¹⁄₂ oz/generous ¹⁄₂ cup/100 g bitter chocolate
2 oz/4 tbsp/50 g butter
2 eggs
3¹⁄₂ oz/generous ¹⁄₃ cup/100 g sugar

Make a dough with the butter, flour, egg, sugar and cocoa. Line an 8 in/20 cm tart pan with the dough and cover the bottom with the marmalade. Peel the pears, cut into quarters and arrange them on the dough.

To make the filling, melt the chocolate and butter over a low heat, set aside to cool. Separate the whites of the eggs and beat them until stiff. Blend together the yolks and sugar. Add the chocolate and egg whites. Pour the mixture over the pears and bake in the oven at 350°F/180°C/Mark 4 for about 40 minutes.

Patate all'alloro

The recipes for this menu can be easily executed within an hour and with readily obtainable ingredients – with the exception of the *fegatelli*, pork liver wrapped in caul, a kind of fat that can be omitted. Of course, the skewers could also be barbecued.

Be sure to use a coarse, country bread for the soup, otherwise it will be mushy. Peas are tasty with a variety of other herbs, Italian parsley and mint, for example, but tarragon is the classic herb of Siena.

Nothing could be more simple than this dessert. Our honey has a pleasingly bitter aftertaste that contrasts nicely with the rich vanilla ice cream but other honeys will also be lovely.

Suggested Wines   Chilled Coltibuono Bianco, a blend of the traditional white grapes of Chianti, Trebbiano and Malvasia, with an addition of Chardonnay, would be my choice with the first course; a young Chianti Classico with the meat; and nothing goes better with the dessert than Coltibuono Vin Santo.

PAPPA AL POMODORO
Bread and tomato soup

8 oz/225 g stale country bread
4 fl oz/1/2 cup/125 ml extra virgin olive oil
2 garlic cloves
2 sage leaves
2 1/4 lb/1 kg ripe plum tomatoes
50 fl oz/6 1/4 cups/1.4 liters broth (page 189)
3 tbsp chopped thyme
salt and pepper

Thinly slice the bread. Pour the oil into a saucepan and add garlic and sage. Sauté until golden. Add the bread, allowing it to absorb the oil for 2 minutes, stirring frequently.

Peel the tomatoes by blanching in boiling water for 1 minute. Rub through a sieve and add to the bread/oil mixture. Cook for 5 minutes. Add the broth and the thyme. Cook over low heat for about 30 minutes, stirring occasionally. Season to taste.

SPIEDINI DI SALSICCE E FEGATELLI
Skewers with pig's liver and sausages

1 caul net, about 20 in/50 cm
6 pieces pig's liver, about 2 oz/50 g each
12 small rectangular slices country bread, about the size of the liver
12 small pork sausages
3 tbsp extra virgin olive oil
6 sprigs fennel
pepper

Soak the caul net in cold water for about 1 hour and drain. Cut in 6 pieces and use to wrap the pieces of liver, securing each with a toothpick.

On each skewer put a slice of bread, a sausage, a piece of liver wrapped in caul, a sausage and another piece of bread. Pepper and brush generously with oil. Stick a sprig of fennel into the liver wrapped in caul.

Pour the rest of the oil into an ovenproof dish, put in the skewers side by side and cook in the oven at 350°F/180°C/Mark 4 for about 1 hour, basting frequently with the cooking juices. When the bread has turned golden and crisp, arrange the skewers of meat on a platter and serve.

PISELLINI ALL'OLIO E DRAGONCELLO
Peas with tarragon and virgin olive oil

1 1/4 lb/5 cups/600 g shelled peas
1 small onion chopped
1 tbsp sugar
2 sprigs tarragon
4 tbsp extra virgin olive oil
1 tbsp chopped parsley
salt and pepper

In a saucepan bring to the boil 1 in/2.5 cm salted water. Add the peas, onion, sugar, tarragon and 1 tablespoon of the oil. Cook for about 5 minutes. Drain and pour in a serving bowl. Add the remaining oil, the parsley and pepper, and serve.

GELATO CON SALSA AL MIELE DI CASTAGNO
Ice cream with chestnut blossom honey

6 egg yolks
35 fl oz/4 1/3 cups/1 liter whipping cream
5 oz/2/3 cup/150 g sugar
7 fl oz/1/2 cup plus 1 tbsp/200 ml honey

Whisk the egg yolks briefly. Heat cream and sugar together, add to the yolks and cook over low heat until the custard coats the spoon, stirring constantly. Freeze according to the instructions for your ice cream maker.

When ready to serve, put the ice cream into 6 glass cups. Heat the honey in a pan and pour it over the ice cream while still boiling hot. Bring to the table immediately.

Spiedini di salsicce e fegatelli
Pappa al pomodoro

MENU FOR A SUNDAY DINNER

MINESTRA D'UOVA
Egg soup

CINGHIALE IN DOLCEFORTE
Wild boar in sweet and sour chocolate sauce

CIPOLLE RIPIENE AGLI AMARETTI
Onions stuffed with amaretti

SORBETTO DI UVA
Grape sorbet

MINESTRA D'UOVA
Egg soup

60 fl oz/7½ cups/1.7 liters chicken broth
4 eggs
2 oz/1 cup/50 g fine dry breadcrumbs
2 oz/½ cup/50 g grated Parmesan cheese
2 fl oz/¼ cup/50 ml lemon juice
grated rind of 1 lemon
salt and pepper
3 tbsp fresh thyme

Bring the broth to the boil in a saucepan. Blend the eggs, breadcrumbs, cheese, lemon juice and rind together in a bowl. Season with salt and pepper to taste.

Turn off the heat under the broth and pour in the egg mixture, blending well with a whisk. Turn on the heat, and stir until the soup comes to the boil. Ladle into soup bowls, garnish with thyme and serve immediately.

CINGHIALE IN DOLCEFORTE
Wild boar in sweet and sour chocolate sauce

3 lb/1.5 kg wild boar or hare, suitable for braising, cut into pieces
2 carrots, roughly chopped
2 celery stalks, roughly chopped
2 yellow onions, roughly chopped
½ bottle good red wine
4 tbsp extra virgin olive oil
1 tsp juniper berries
2 bay leaves
salt
1 tsp black peppercorns
2 oz/¼ cup/50 g sugar
4 cloves garlic, coarsely chopped
4 fl oz/½ cup/125 ml red wine vinegar
2 oz/2 squares/50 g grated bitter chocolate
2 oz/⅓ cup/50 g raisins soaked in water
2 oz/½ cup/50 g stoned (pitted) dried prunes, soaked in water

With the exception of the soup (which only requires a couple of minutes of cooking time), this impressive autumnal menu can all be prepared ahead of time so that you can relax and enjoy your guests. Both the first and last courses are light and refreshing and set off well the rather sumptuous, savory main and side dishes. I like to garnish and serve the soup in individual cups. The sweet and sour chocolate sauce goes well with other strong-flavored game, such as hare and venison, or even with well-hung beef. The blending of strong and contrasting flavors in this dish, as well as in the onions and amaretti, was typical of the cooking of the Renaissance.

For additional elegance, scoop out the sorbet in little balls and arrange in a grape bunch. The sorbet is also delightful topped with a sauce of fresh berries.

Suggested Wines Coltibuono Rosato is lovely with the soup. The wild boar calls for a rich, full-bodied red. I would choose one of our Chianti Classico Riservas, perhaps the 1968, or Sangioveto di Coltibuono with its subtle oak aroma. Serve a glass of Coltibuono Grappa with the dessert and invite your guests to pour a little over the sorbet. It is delicious!

Cipolle ripiene agli amaretti

2 oz/¼ cup/50 g pine nuts

1 tbsp finely chopped candied citron

Twenty-four hours ahead, put the meat in a good-sized flameproof casserole together with the carrots, celery and onions. Add the wine and marinate for 24 hours, turning the meat from time to time.

On the serving day, remove the meat from the marinade, pat dry. In a large skillet, heat the olive oil until it begins to color. Brown the meat on all sides. Strain the vegetables from the marinade, add to the meat with the juniper berries, 1 of the bay leaves, salt and pepper. Pour some of the marinade over. Cover and simmer for 1½ hours or until the meat is tender, adding the remaining marinade, a little at a time.

Transfer the meat to a flameproof casserole. Purée the vegetables, then pour them over the meat and reheat. In a saucepan, melt the sugar with the garlic and remaining bay leaf, and cook until lightly colored. Add the vinegar and bitter chocolate. Boil for a few minutes. Add the sauce to the meat together with the raisins, prunes, pine nuts and candied citron. Simmer together for 10 minutes before serving.

CIPOLLE RIPIENE AGLI AMARETTI
Onions stuffed with amaretti

6 medium red onions

12 amaretti biscuits (cookies)

1 handful Italian bread, soaked in milk and squeezed dry

1 egg

pinch of grated nutmeg

salt and pepper

1 oz/2 tbsp/25 g butter

Boil the onions in water until tender but not mushy. Cut in half. Take out the insides, leaving the root end intact, and ¼ in/0.5 cm on the sides. Allow to cool.

Crush the amaretti and mix with the bread,

Sorbetto di uva

egg, nutmeg, salt and pepper. Fill the onions to the top with the mixture and dot with butter. Butter a baking dish. Set the stuffed onions in the dish, then bake in the oven at 350°F/180°C/Mark 4 for about 40 minutes.

SORBETTO DI UVA
Grape sorbet

3¼ lb/1.5 kg red grapes

8 fl oz/1 cup/225 ml water

4 oz/½ cup/125 g sugar

3 tbsp lemon juice

1 egg white

Gently simmer the grapes with the water and sugar for 10 minutes until soft. Pass through a food mill and cool in an icewater bath. Add the lemon juice. Place in freezer or put in an ice cream machine. When frozen, break into chunks, put in a food processor with the egg white and blend until creamy. Refreeze and serve.

SARDEGNA

CASA GUISO A OROSEI

*Food for a religious folk festival at the ancestral
home of Don Giovanni Guiso*

We could, of course, fly but the only really satisfactory way to travel to an island is by sea and the boat trip to Sardegna is very easy and most enjoyable. The best time to make the journey is at night. The ship leaves the Italian mainland a little before midnight and shortly after dawn the next day you are sailing into the harbor of Olbia, a port on the east coast of the island. The cabin attendants awaken you about 5 a.m., just in time to see the vague shapes of massive promontories that rise out of the sea through the lifting darkness, the first foreshadowing of the mystery that seems to envelop this island, casting its enticing spell over everything and everyone. Some seventy years ago, D. H. Lawrence wrote that going to Sardegna is like going nowhere, so outside the circuit of European civilization did

*The small flotilla of decorated fishing boats which leave Orosei for the chapel of Santa Maria 'e Mare
on the mouth of the Cedrino river, and above, the interior of the chapel itself*

105

he find it. Well, a lot has changed since then but fortunately much of that "otherness" still remains.

We are going to the village of Orosei, about midway down the eastern coast, to visit my dear friend, Don Giovanni Guiso, at his ancestral home. It is the last weekend of May and every year at this time under his patronage the religious folk festival in honor of the Madonna, Santa Maria 'e Mare (Saint Mary of the Sea) is celebrated.

Thus far during the course of this tour we have encountered various manifestations of a renaissance, old and new, and now I am going to introduce you to a Renaissance man. Don Giovanni, Nanni, as he is called by his friends, is really quite extraordinary, a personality with many facets and all of them brilliant. He was born in Orosei, where for centuries his ancestors were the barons of the surrounding territory, an area of Sardegna traditionally called the *Baronia*. Here he spent the first twenty years of his life before leaving for Rome to study law. He chose Siena to begin his practice because he felt it a place whose spirit was congenial to his own, a city still of human proportions, elegant and refined and a lively center of culture and the arts.

For the feast, mass is said outside the chapel.
The fishermen, dressed in traditional Sardinian costumes,
sing the Lord's prayer in dialect

In his adopted hometown, Nanni lives in a very special apartment, the top floor of a medieval palace with five bay windows overlooking the Piazza del Campo, one of the most beautiful open spaces in the world, which he modestly calls the "courtyard" of his home. He has decorated the comfortable and easy elegance of its interiors with his collection of fine drawings, including a prized Picasso.

In his splendid Renaissance villa just a few miles outside of Siena, Nanni has assembled another collection that is his life-long passion, over thirty miniature theaters, some toys, other eighteenth-century shadow boxes and one, almost life size. He especially delights in staging marionette operatic performances for his friends. I shall always remember a New Year's Eve production of excerpts from *Tosca*. The costumes and sets were designed for the occasion by Sir Peter Hall and made in the workshops of the Metropolitan Opera in New York. Callas sang Tosca and Giuseppe di Stefano, Cavaradossi. A recording, of course, but with Nanni pulling the strings and creating the illusion, who even noticed?

The feast of Santa Maria 'e Mare is a dramatic spectacle of another kind directed by Nanni. It all began almost fifteen years ago in response to a letter written by Giuseppina Manca, a teacher at the elementary school of Orosei, and her pupils, asking Nanni and his brother if they would consider restoring the family's ancient chapel of Santa Maria 'e Mare. It stood partially in ruins on a plateau about a mile from the town where the Cedrino river winds gently into the sea. Nanni's ancestors had built the chapel and for centuries the wives of the fishermen of Orosei had come to pray to the Madonna for the safety of their husbands. During the last war it had been used as a military installation and afterward was virtually forgotten.

Nanni devoted himself to the project with his characteristic intelligence and enthusiasm and two years later the chapel had been restored to its original simplicity and its lovely

walled garden flourished. Even the small, marvelously crafted, votive ships that had been left over the years in thanksgiving for answered prayers once again adorned the walls and arches of the sanctuary. Not only did he restore her chapel, he also revived the traditional annual feast-day celebration in honor of Santa Maria 'e Mare.

Nanni always invites a congenial group of about twenty friends to spend the weekend of the feast at his family home, a seventeenth-century house built of whitewashed clay and stone, originally the ancestral homes of his grandfather and grandmother joined together on the occasion of their marriage. The interiors are decorated in a marvelous mélange of styles of various origins and epochs that reflect the travels abroad of his parents and grandparents as well as his own endeavors to collect rare Sardinian pieces. But it is in the immense courtyard that I most enjoy spending my leisurely hours at Orosei, under the shade of the enormous palm tree that dominates this enchanting space where bougainvillaea, cactus, geraniums, oleander and numerous other flowers and plants bloom in abundance. Their scent and color is almost overwhelming. In fact, when a friend of mine asked the local policeman standing in the village square directions to Nanni's house, he was told to take the first street to the left, follow it up the hill until he smelled the fragrance of blooming jasmine and there he would find the domain of Don Giovanni Guiso.

Over the centuries many illustrious guests have been entertained here. Sardinians are a people renowned for their hospitality and in what had been until relatively recently a wild and primitive area of the island, the Guiso home was the only place were important guests of the realm could be received in comfort. D. H. Lawrence passed through while he was writing *Sea and Sardinia*. His reaction to Orosei was characteristically ambiguous. Upon arriving he describes it as "a dilapidated, sun-smitten, god-forsaken little town . . . with

Casa Guiso

a few grumpy inhabitants who won't even give you a crust of bread." When leaving, he waxes lyrical, writing, "Oh, wonderful Orosei with your almonds and your reedy river, throbbing, throbbing with light and the sea's nearness, and all so lost, in a world long gone by, lingering as legends linger on." One would like to think that it was a good lunch and a bottle of wine at the Guiso home that accounts for his change in mood.

And at Nanni's one does eat very well, indeed. Besides so many other qualities, he is also a gastronome and is president of the Siena chapter of the *Accademia della Cucina*. For Nanni's guests the festivities start with Saturday supper on the eve of the feast-day. The meal begins with a delicious version of one of the many bread soups typical of Sardegna. Alternate layers of peasant bread and shepherd's cheese are baked in a lamb's broth seasoned with fresh fennel seeds.

For the main course, according to a now well-established tradition, Nanni serves *aragosta* or rock lobster. Sardegna is reputed to be blessed with Italy's richest harvest of fish, both from the still unpolluted waters of the surrounding sea and from its fresh mountain streams, and its *aragosta* are the most succulent in the Mediterranean. A local restaurateur left at 3.30 a.m. in the morning to drive to a fisherman's market in a village further down the coast in order to get them "still kicking," as he put it. This aristocrat of shellfish is often seen tarted up in all kinds of fancy dress but the noble specimens from these waters need no disguise. Bernardina, Nanni's cook, prepares them freshly boiled, seasoned with a simple sauce based on olive oil, salt and a few drops of lemon.

Local confectionery

Giuseppina, who, since that fateful letter has become a close friend of Nanni and his right hand for organizing the *festa*, has brought a specialty from her native city, nearby Nuoro, for dessert. These are cookies made of sugar, almonds and honey and decorated with exquisite rococo designs in white frosting. Some are in the form of little hearts (*cuoricini*) and others have been cut out in the shape of flowers, animals and sea shells. Each region of Sardegna uses its own imagination with regard to the form and decoration of these cookies and bake them for the important feast-days of the year.

On the following morning there is the inauguration of an exhibition of books illustrated by famous artists of the cubist period which Nanni has organized in order to provide a cultural dimension to this traditionally religious folk festival. All the dignitaries of the surrounding area are present and invited back to the villa for a buffet luncheon afterward. The menu features some of my favorite regional dishes.

Two traditional types of pasta are served for the first course, a characteristic gnocchi named *malloreddus* and *macarones de busa*, a hand-rolled, slender spaghetti. Both are made without eggs but with much loving care in the kneading and are served with two different types of fresh herbal sauce. Genuine *malloreddus* like these, made in a Sardinian home, carry a mark of authenticity: little designs embossed in the dough by pressing it with the thumb against the inner ribbing of the classical handwoven Sardinian basket.

What would a visit to Sardegna be without tasting fresh sardines, the tiny fish that took its name from this island? The ones that are the main course for today's meal are baked in breadcrumbs, olive oil and parsley and are served with slices of baked aubergine (egg-plant,) seasoned with marjoram and tomato sauce.

For dessert Bernardina treats us to one of those regional specialties that in itself merit the trip. It is called *sebada* or sometimes *seada* and features a juxtaposition of ingredients that at first might seem like strange bedfellows, cheese and honey. Balls of sheep cheese are rolled in flour, deep-fried and while still piping hot served with an aromatic wild honey poured over them. Cool Cannonau wine, a slightly sweet rosato from Nanni's own vineyard, is a delicious accompaniment for the entire luncheon.

And now it is almost time for the principal event of the *festa* to begin. Down at the bridge over the Cedrino river that runs below the village, a veritable fleet of small fishing boats is gathering. Each one is decorated with bright pergolas of wild flowers and manned by a fisherman, looking proud and splendid in black linen breeches and white billowy shirt with a bright red vest. They are accompanied in their boats by a bevy of women, who are also dressed in traditional Sardinian garb, skirts of vermilion cloth with embroidered bands at the bottom and beautifully embroidered blouses.

In one of these boats, not decorated with a pergola so that everyone can see her and instead draped with scarlet bunting, will ride the most important passenger of all, the statue of Santa Maria 'e Mare, a copy of the original seventeenth-century life-size image kept in the chapel. I have been invited to ride with Nanni and his family in a lesser VIP boat.

About 5 p.m. the boat procession starts out on its leisurely hour's journey to the chapel of Santa Maria 'e Mare. There are about fifteen processional boats in all, with several joiners bringing up the rear of the cortege. They are a lovely sight to behold winding through the marshes, merging in and out of the branches of the willow trees that line the river banks. Many inhabitants of Orosei follow the boat procession on foot. These are mostly women and a good number of them seem to be the widows of the village, handsome and looking curiously chic, given today's fashion, dressed totally in black from head to toe. Now the fishermen begin to chant ancient hymns in honor of the Madonna. Theirs is a strange, somewhat haunting monotone and the words in Sardinian dialect seem exotic with hispanic and arabic sounds. The men are answered by the women walking along the road that skirts the bank. Their chant is less staccato, more legato, with a sound that sometimes swells, and a beautiful rhythm is established along the way between the rowing and the chanting and the walking in procession.

When we arrive almost at the point where the river meets the sea, the procession carrying the Madonna in her shrine winds up the hill to the chapel. By now there must be several hundred people, come from neighboring towns and villages, who assemble in the garden for the celebration of Mass. Again the fishermen chant their hymns, this time led by a cantor with a sweet tenor voice.

Meanwhile, down along the moorland between the river and the sea, men are preparing large open fires of charcoal for the biggest fish-fry I have ever seen. They turn the fish on the grill with a kind of large rake. The variety is vast and I recognize gray mullet, sea bream and an occasional trout from the Cedrino. *Polpi*, small Mediterranean octopus, seem to be the featured fish on the menu. Another specialty of this feast are shellfish salad sandwiches. The salad consists of every imaginable variety of crustacean and this is heaped on large slices of coarse peasant bread. In days gone by it was Nanni's family who supplied the fish, but now it is all donated by the local fishermen in thanksgiving to Santa Maria 'e Mare for the plentiful yield of her Sardinian sea and for the safety of the men who fish her waters.

There is also plenty of wine for all (Nanni's gift) and the inevitable vendors of carnival candies and other sweets have set up their stalls along the road. As night falls the dancing begins but disco dominates even on these

Drawing room interior, Casa Guiso

remote shores, so we decide to leave before the spell of this enchanting day is broken.

Early the next morning the few friends who are staying to catch the night boat back to the mainland set out with Nanni for a picnic in a most extraordinary place. The car can take us only part of the way, so we leave it on a moor near the sea and begin to climb by foot up a rocky cliff. Soon we reach a grassy spot and there it is, Nanni's *nuraghe* – a prehistoric habitation, peculiar to Sardegna and especially to this part of the island, constructed as a fortification from enormous blocks of cut stone. Nanni's is on a plot of land that has been owned by his family for generations. Here the terrain drops clifflike to the water and one enjoys a spectacular view of the sea beyond.

But there is yet another surprise in store. Vittorio, Bernardina's husband, has been up here since dawn preparing the main course for

our picnic lunch. It is *the* delicacy of the island, *porceddu*, roast suckling pig. First he had to dig the pit for the fire, over which the milk-fed piglet, covered with sprigs of myrtle, has slowly been roasting on a vertical spit. From the village baker Bernardina has brought stacks of flat, unleavened bread called *carta da musica* (music paper) because of its thin texture.

As Sardinian herdsmen have done for centuries we sit ourselves down in sight of the *nuraghe* and eat *porceddu* between pieces of *carta da musica* (Caterina de'Medici's knives and forks have no place here.) And for a moment, at least, we feel ourselves outside of time and civilization.

Back home, however, I have a problem to resolve. I want to send Nanni a gift of appreciation for such a wonderful weekend. But what can you give to the man who has everything – even a *nuraghe*!

MENU FOR A SARDINIAN SUPPER

ZUPPA D'AGNELLO
Lamb and pecorino soup

ARAGOSTA DELLA BERNARDINA
Lobster with olive oil and herb sauce

FAVE CON CICORIA
Broad beans (fava beans) with curly endive

CROCCANTINI DI NUORO
Crunchy biscuits (cookies)

Aragosta is such a delicious delicacy that other dishes on the menu ought to leave space for it to reign supreme. Above all, the accompanying sauce should only heighten and never hide its exquisite flavor. Because the soup is low in liquid, it is less filling than it may sound and the delicate taste of the fresh fennel adds a touch of refinement as well as stimulating the appetite. The leg of lamb can be used again on the following day for making croquettes mixed with mashed potatoes, cheese and some parsley for seasoning. The curly endive with the beans also has an agreeably sharp and stimulating flavor and the biscuits are light and lovely to look at.

Suggested Wines With the soup and lobster serve a fruity white wine such as a Vermentino. There is even one made called Aragosta. The island produces several fine dessert wines. Malvasia di Bosa with its suggestion of toasted almonds is the ideal accompaniment for the cookies.

ZUPPA D'AGNELLO
Lamb and pecorino soup

1 leg of lamb
1 carrot
1 celery stalk
1 small onion
1 bunch wild fennel (or 1 fennel bulb)
100 fl oz/12½ cups/3 liters water
salt and pepper
12 thin slices Italian-style bread
12 very thin slices fresh sheep's cheese (pecorino)

Cut the leg of lamb in half and place in a large saucepan. Clean and roughly chop the vegetables and add to the pan with half the fennel, the water, salt and pepper. Bring to the boil, and cook over low heat for 2 hours. Strain the broth, and leave to cool, then remove the fat that will have formed on the surface.

Place alternating slices of bread and cheese in a baking dish. Pour the stock over and bake for 20 minutes in the oven at 350°F/180°C/Mark 4. Finely chop the remaining fennel, and sprinkle it over the soup before serving.

ARAGOSTA DELLA BERNARDINA
Lobster with olive oil and herb sauce

140 fl oz/4½ quarts/4 liters water
1 bottle dry white wine
3 live lobsters about 2¼ lb/1 kg each
salt and pepper
12 tbsp extra virgin olive oil
1 tbsp chopped basil
juice of ½ lemon
2 cloves garlic
4 walnuts, chopped
2 tbsp pine nuts
2 anchovy fillets in oil

Put the water and wine in a large pan, add a little salt and bring to the boil. Add the lobsters, cook for about 20 minutes, then drain. Meanwhile, put the remaining ingre-

dients in a food processor and mix to a smooth sauce.

Remove the meat from the lobsters, being careful to preserve as much of the shape of the bottom part of the shell as possible. Slice the meat into pieces and return to the shell. Serve the sauce separately.

FAVE CON CICORIA
Broad beans (fava beans) with curly endive

6½ lb/3 kg broad beans (fava beans), shelled
10 oz/300 g (1 very small head) curly endive
salt and pepper
3 ripe tomatoes
4 tbsp extra virgin olive oil

Cook the beans and curly endive in a pan of boiling, salted water for 5 minutes, then drain. Squeeze the endive dry and chop roughly. Peel the transparent skin from the beans.

Peel and chop the tomatoes. Salt and drain. Heat the olive oil in a casserole, add the beans and endive, cover and cook over low heat for about 10 minutes. Add the tomatoes, pepper and continue to heat, uncovered, for a couple more minutes. Pour into a dish and serve.

CROCCANTINI DI NUORO
Crunchy cookies

14 oz/2¾ cups/400 g blanched almonds
9 oz/1¼ cups/250 g granulated sugar
7 oz/1¾ cups/200 g icing (confectioners') sugar
3 tbsp water
1 tbsp almond oil

Preheat the oven to 400°F/200°C/Mark 6. Roast the almonds until golden brown, then chop finely. Caramelize the granulated sugar in a heavy pan, being careful not to let it turn too dark. Mix in the roasted almonds and pour onto a flat surface greased with almond oil.

Croccantini di Nuoro

MENU FOR A SARDINIAN SUNDAY LUNCHEON

MALLOREDDUS E MACARONES
·DE BUSA
Saffron gnocchi and thin tubular spaghetti with
a ricotta sauce

SARDE AL PANGRATTATO
Fresh sardines baked in breadcrumbs

MELANZANE AL POMODORO
Aubergines (eggplant) with fresh tomato sauce

SEBADAS
Deep-fried cheese discs with honey

As is common on southern Italian menus, the mainstay of this meal is the pasta course. It is quite difficult to form the spaghetti the authentic way, with a knitting needle, but commercial pasta of the *bucatini* type is a satisfactory substitute. The gnocchi are quite simple to make, and an adequate imitation of the traditional decoration can be had by pressing the prongs of a fork against the dough. The classic sauce with these pastas is fresh tomato, but this one of ricotta is very Sardinian.

In various parts of Italy sardines are prepared in a variety of ways, but this recipe is the most simple and tasty. If the aubergines (eggplant) are fresh and young there is no need to go through that ritual of salting and draining, which robs them of their flavor and tends to make them mushy.

As a variation on the sebadas, try grilling (broiling) a slice of firm, young pecorino until it becomes slightly brown and bubbly and then top with honey.

Suggested Wines This is a fine meal for a chilled rosé. Cannonau di Sardegna Rosato is a good choice, a sweet version of which is also delicious with the sebadas.

Quickly spread the mixture to a thickness of about ⅛ in/0.25 cm. Before it hardens completely, using a biscuit (cookie) cutter greased with almond oil, cut into little hearts (or other shapes).

Mix the icing (confectioners') sugar with the water until it takes on the consistency of thick cream. Using a piping (pastry) bag with the narrowest nozzle possible, decorate the biscuits with a lace-style design. Serve on a platter.

Malloreddus e macarones de busa

SARDE AL PANGRATTATO
Fresh sardines baked in breadcrumbs

2¼ lb/1 kg fresh sardines
6 tbsp extra virgin olive oil
4 oz/1 cup/125 g finely grated dry breadcrumbs
2 tbsp chopped Italian parsley
salt and pepper

Remove the sardine heads. Cut open the sardines and remove the backbones, leaving the tails on. Wash and dry. Grease a round baking dish with some of the olive oil and put in the sardines. Sprinkle with breadcrumbs, parsley, salt and pepper. Drizzle over the remaining olive oil, and cook in the oven at 400°F/200°C/Mark 6 for 20 minutes and serve.

MELANZANE AL POMODORO
Aubergines (eggplant) with fresh tomato sauce

1 small onion
2 cloves garlic
3 tbsp extra virgin olive oil
2¼ lb/1 kg ripe plum tomatoes
2 tbsp chopped tarragon
3 large oval-shaped aubergines (eggplant)
10 oz/300 g mozzarella cheese
salt and pepper
8 leaves fresh basil

Chop the onion and the garlic. Heat the oil in a saucepan and sauté the onion and garlic over low heat until transparent. Peel and roughly chop the tomatoes and add to the saucepan together with the tarragon. Cook until the liquid is completely reduced.

Cut the aubergines (eggplant) into 18 slices about ½ in/1 cm thick. Cook under a grill (broiler) for a few minutes, turning once. Place the slices on a piece of foil and top each one with a thin slice of mozzarella and a dab of the sauce. Cook in the oven at 400°F/200°C/Mark 6 for 5 minutes. Arrange on a platter, season, decorate with the basil and serve.

MALLOREDDUS E MACARONES DE BUSA
Saffron gnocchi and thin tubular spaghetti with a ricotta sauce

18 oz/3½ cups/500 g semolina flour
4 fl oz/½ cup/125 ml water
10 oz/1¼ cups/300 g ricotta cheese
pinch of powdered saffron
2 tbsp finely chopped parsley
6 tbsp extra virgin olive oil

Make a dough by mixing the flour and water, working it for at least 10 minutes until it becomes smooth and elastic. Form into a ball, then cover with a bowl to keep moist until ready to use (page 188). Roll out the dough in 2 thin sheets. To make the gnocchi, cut off small pieces of the dough, about the size of a hazelnut, and press each one against the prongs on the inside curve of a fork. To make the spaghetti, roll pieces of extra thin dough around a knitting needle. Bring to the boil 2 large saucepans of salted water and cook separately the 2 types of pasta until *al dente*.

To make the sauce, mix 6 tbsp of the pasta water with the ricotta and divide into 2 equal portions. Dissolve the saffron with another tablespoon of pasta water and mix with half the ricotta. Mix the parsley with the other half. Heat the 2 ricotta sauces in separate double boilers.

Drain the pasta and divide between 2 serving bowls, mixing in the olive oil. Pour the saffron sauce over the gnocchi and the parsley sauce over the spaghetti.

Sebadas

SEBADAS
Deep-fried cheese discs with honey

7 oz/200 g very fresh pecorino (or Swiss) cheese
1 tbsp semolina flour
10 oz/2 cups/300 g plain (all-purpose) flour
1 oz/2 tbsp/25 g lard
oil for frying
7 fl oz/1/2 cup plus 1 tbsp/200 g slightly bitter honey, preferably chestnut blossom

Put the cheese in a saucepan with the semolina flour and a little water. Melt over a low heat until a dense cream is formed. Remove from the heat. Moisten the palms of your hands, and using about a tablespoon at a time, form the melted cheese into thin discs.

Make a dough with the flour, lard and water, working it until it becomes smooth and elastic. Roll out into 2 thin sheets as if making pasta. At a regular distance on the surface of 1 sheet place the discs of cheese. Cover with the second piece of dough and seal, eliminating any air inside. Using a pastry cutter, divide again into discs about 4 in/10 cm in diameter.

Fry the discs, a few at a time, in very hot oil and drain on paper towels. Arrange on a platter, pour over the honey and serve while still hot.

There is, of course, no substitute for cooking your picnic over a charcoal fire. However, if that is not possible, the shellfish salad is the makings of a super-deluxe sandwich, an appetizing beach lunch in itself. The roast pig is delicious cold, when the rosemary, bay and garlic have thoroughly flavored it.

Any accompaniment to these picnic dishes should be simple and easy. To go with the fish, bring along a bowl of fresh new potatoes, boiled in their skins, mixed with melted butter and finely chopped parsley, or a salad of crisp *fagiolini* (green beans) seasoned with salt, olive oil and lemon juice. With the pork, a garden lettuce salad with lots of rocket (arugula) is best. Serve hunks of country-style bread with the fish and a thin, crisp *focaccia* to eat with the suckling pig. For dessert, serve fresh fruit – cherries or perfectly ripe melon – and dry, crunchy Italian almond biscuits (cookies) to dip in your wine.

Suggested Wines Bring to the beach a Nuraghe majore, a delicately scented, crisp white, named after Sardinia's prehistoric stone towers. With the roast pig, try a red Cannonau superiore, dry and hearty. Sardegna makes several types of Moscato you could try with the fruit and biscuits (cookies).

INSALATA DI MOLLUSCHI
Shellfish salad

½ bottle rosé or white wine

1 bunch parsley plus 2 tbsp chopped parsley

2¼ lb/1 kg scallops

2¼ lb/1 kg baby clams

2¼ lb/1 kg mussels

2¼ lb/1 kg sea dates
(or any other type of small shellfish)

salt and pepper

juice of 1 lemon

8 tbsp extra virgin olive oil

Divide the wine and the bunch of parsley among four saucepans for each type of shellfish. Add the shellfish, bring to boil and cook until the shells open. Drain and remove the meat from the shells, discarding any shells that remain closed. Reserve 3 tbsp of the strained cooking liquid.

In a saucepan, dissolve the salt in the lemon juice. Add the chopped parsley, olive oil, pepper and the strained clam broth. Mix the shellfish on a platter, pour over the olive oil mixture and serve.

POLPO ALLA GRIGLIA
Grilled octopus

juice of 1 lemon

4 tbsp extra virgin olive oil

salt and pepper

2¼ lb/1 kg octopus

Mix the lemon juice, olive oil, salt and pepper. Discard the beak and eyes of the octopus and pound the flesh until it becomes tender. Cut in half lengthwise and marinate in the olive oil mixture for at least 2 hours.

Grill the octopus over a hot charcoal fire for about 10 minutes, turning frequently and brushing with the marinade. Cut into bite-sized pieces and serve.

PORCEDDU
Roast suckling pig

1 handful garlic cloves

several sprigs rosemary and bay leaves

6½ lb/3 kg suckling pig

1 handful salt

Chop the garlic and rosemary, mix with the salt, then rub well into the skin of the piglet. Stuff the meat with the bay leaves and tie the legs firmly.

Roast in a preheated oven at 350°F/180°C/Mark 4 for about 1½ hours, then increase the temperature to 400°F/200°C/Mark 6 and cook for 10 minutes, or until the meat takes on color and the skin becomes crackly. Remove the bay leaves, cut into slices and serve.

Porceddu

UMBRIA

LA CANONICA A TODI

*Colorful cooking in a monastic hermitage, home of
abstract artist Piero Dorazio and his wife Giuliana*

Umbria can be tricky territory for a Tuscan to travel through. A certain diplomacy is necessary. I do not think anyone would dispute that these two neighboring areas are the most beautiful rural regions in all of Italy. What is, however, passionately and endlessly discussed, at least by Umbrians and Tuscans, native or naturalized, is which is the most beautiful.

They enjoy many similarities, in their physical as well as in their cultural features. Each is a highly civilized place with a luminous landscape that is both cultivated and wild. Umbria, like Toscana, is studded with stunning hilltop towns full of architectural splendors – Perugia, Orvieto, Assisi, Gubbio, Spoleto, Todi. It, too, has produced great artists – Piero della Francesca, Signorelli, Perugino, Pinturicchio. Both make wonderful wines and fine extra virgin olive oils and produce a cuisine whose excellence is due most of all to the high quality and freshness of the indigenous ingredients, simply and sagely prepared.

*A monastery church on the outskirts of Todi floats above the
autumn morning mists and above, La Canonica*

Across Umbrian tiles towards Todi

In spirit, however, they differ decisively. The two form the heartland of Italy, but Umbria is the green heart, more yielding than Toscana, which can sometimes have a certain harshness. Perhaps because it is the only region on the Italian peninsula that does not open out to the sea, Umbria has a sense of solitude and serenity that I do not feel in garrulous Toscana. Then, too, the fact that the capital cities of the Tuscan provinces are mainly large commercial centers whereas those of Umbria are smaller and favor artisan creativity, gives it a more easy-going atmosphere. And it is no accident that the great Renaissance humanists (and bankers!) came out of fifteenth-century Toscana, nor that San Francesco d'Assisi was born in Umbria. The spirituality of Umbria is a lighthearted yet elevated mysticism, whereas the Tuscan genius has always been more at home within the human dimension. No one

who knows and loves the "*maledetti toscani*" (as even they, with a certain pride, call themselves) could ever imagine the "*poverello*" of Assisi coming out of their ranks!

My Umbrian neighbor, the internationally renowned abstract painter, Piero Dorazio, left his native Roma almost twenty years ago and moved to Umbria primarily because he found there a form of rural community that scarcely, if at all, exists in Toscana. In the hills outside of the ancient and picturesque town of Todi where he and his Milanese wife, Giuliana, have their small farm, they are surrounded with neighbors who own and work their land and take pride in what they produce. This agricultural environment of small-scale farming creates a quality of life lacking in Toscana, where traditionally the land was owned by a relatively few aristocratic families and farmed under a semifeudal share-cropping system.

After the war when the established order broke down, the peasants left the land for the town, and the small farm with the type of civilization it generates virtually disappeared from the Tuscan landscape.

Besides extensive olive groves and vineyards (from which they make and bottle their own wine), the Dorazio keep a small menagerie of farm animals – pigs, goats, geese, chickens, turkeys, guinea fowl – as well as cultivating a large kitchen garden and fruit orchard. What they do not produce themselves, they can easily find freshly made close by. There is a woman in the village who makes fresh bread in an ancient brick oven, a family of shepherds not far off who make pecorino cheese, the local fishmonger from the nearby lake who brings a fresh catch of salmon trout (and on request even a fresh salmon flown in from Scotland,) the ubiquitous Umbrian hunter with an extra hare or two to sell, as well as someone just back from Norcia with his sack full of black truffles who knows that here he will find good customers for this Umbrian delicacy.

Giuliana manages a household that is an expression of their country-life bounty. There is literally something always cooking in the kitchen. I remember once dropping by unexpectedly and finding Annetta, the family cook for almost twenty years, making gnocchi while a whole lamb was spit-roasting on the kitchen fire. When I asked Giuliana who was invited for lunch, she said no one; there was just herself and Piero and their youngest daughter, but someone was sure to come by – and there I was. By lunch time we were seven, not counting several deliverymen who were enjoying a snack of prosciutto and salami *panini* that Annetta had prepared for them in the kitchen. This is normal at the Dorazio home where an integral part of daily life is welcoming friends to the family table.

Giuliana likes to think of this open-door hospitality as a perpetuation of the original spirit of their house. La Canonica, as it is called, was an ancient monastery and in keeping with the best of monastic tradition, friends who arrive are still nourished and cared for before resuming their journey. The Camaldolesi, whose monastery it was, are a unique religious order in the Western world, a group of hermit-monks who construct their monasteries with the chapel and community buildings at the center, surrounded by individual hermitages, each with its enclosed garden. Of these only two of La Canonica's original seventeen remain, and they are now guest cottages. The sprawling, ocher-colored community buildings are the family residence and Piero has transformed the central chapel with its small bell tower still in working order into a studio. This is a splendid baroque space flooded with light whose high, wide walls are ideal for his luminous and immense mural-like paintings.

Not far from Piero's studio there is the other creative center of the Dorazio houshold, Giuliana's kitchen. Here the walls are covered with antique wooden cooking utensils and baskets collected on trips around the world. At its center is a raised fireplace for grilling and spit-roasting, where Annetta keeps the fire going all year round. Off the kitchen is the dining room with a long refectory table where there is always room to add another place for the unexpected guest. It is often set with majolica plates and wine glasses decorated with Piero's characteristic network of colorful lines crossing over one another in subtle weaves – a motif that is repeated on his wine label.

It is not just for the benefit of guests that their table is laid. One gets the impression that sitting down to a good meal in good company is important to Piero, almost a ritual. A painter's life is inevitably solitary and when Piero emerges from his studio at lunch time he seems to take sustenance from both the food and the conversation.

The combination of Dorazio hospitality and

Giuliana has a passion for collecting wooden kitchen utensils which cover every available inch of the walls

the four-seasons' abundance of Umbria makes any time a very good time to visit La Canonica. In spring, for example, wild asparagus proliferates on the surrounding hills. At the height of the season it is not unusual to come across young boys selling bunches of these *asparagi di campo* on the roadside. Annetta freezes enough to last almost the year. Fresh, it is exquisite simply boiled for only a couple of minutes and dressed with olive oil, pepper and lemon juice. The tips tossed in very thin spaghetti with just some fruity Umbrian olive oil and freshly ground pepper added is a perfect springtime pasta. A favorite way to enjoy asparagus at the Dorazio table is as a filling for a *frittata*. This Italian omelet is quick and easy to make, tasty hot or cold, and a good way to augment a menu should there be a last-minute increase in the number of guests.

While the wives picked the wild asparagus, their husbands used to go on a pigeon shoot. Understandably these wild pigeons changed their migratory route – but only to find themselves under even heavier fire in Toscana. Even though they can no longer be found in the woods of Umbria, this feathered game is still a specialty on the table. Traditionally they are roasted on the spit before a wood fire until

*Umbria is famed for its decorated pottery.
These plates are made at Deruta*

partly cooked and then leisurely simmered in a pan with olive oil and plenty of robust Umbrian red wine. Annetta also pot-roasts them in the classical Umbrian *salsa ghiotta*, a sauce made with prosciutto and herbs.

In summer, meals at La Canonica are usually enjoyed *al fresco* under the shade of a vine arbor in the lush and rambling gardens enclosed within the ancient cloister walls. Fish is most frequently on the table during this season. Umbria has several lakes and fresh mountain streams and the region's trout is particularly excellent. Piero takes a personal interest in cooking these. His recipe is to bake them in foil with rosemary, thyme, bay, parsley, garlic, olive oil – and any other herb that his artistic intuition suggests at the moment. Annetta prefers to grill them, their insides stuffed with herbs and with a couple of capers added. Chicken is another summertime specialty. Tuscans like to think that theirs are the best but I have never tasted any better than one of the Dorazio's free-range fowl perfectly roasted on the spit. Annetta cooks the versatile chicken breast rubbed with olive paste. I like to roll these and baste them frequently with milk while they slowly cook.

Umbria saves her gastronomic grand finale for autumn and early winter when the countryside produces three outstanding events. First comes grape harvest. Umbria grows an amazing variety of vines from which it produces a wealth of wines. Piero makes a white called Setteuve, a blend of seven grape varieties, and a red, Scacciadiavoli (which literally means "cast out devils"), a blend of five grapes, including cabernet and merlot, and aged in barriques for three years. Harvest at La Canonica lasts a week and between family, friends and professional pickers, Annetta and her helpers prepare a daily midday repast for some seventy hungry workers. The menu is simple and substantial, usually two types of pasta and large platters of assorted roasted meats. One pasta I particularly enjoy is made with a sauce of black olives. At home I add

orange peel. It is not only fast, easy and flavorful but also colorful. Usually around grape-harvest time, under the first early-autumn rains, a wide variety of mushrooms spring up, especially in the hills wooded with beech and chestnut trees. When the autumn evenings turn chilly, Giuliana serves a piping hot mushroom pie made with a simple pastry crust and filled with porcini sautéd in olive oil and butter. It is perfect either for a first course or as the main dish for a light supper.

The second notable event of this season is the arrival of the celebrated black truffle. Usually by late November or early December one can see the Umbrian farmer set off into the woods around Spoleto and Norcia with his trusty truffle hound. In a good season they return with a sackful of warty ebony tubers. The Umbrian black truffle I find richer in flavor than its more aristocratic cousins from Piemonte, although not as powerful or penetrating in scent.

They are highly esteemed even in France where, it is said, many of them end up in the *foie gras* of Perigord and Strasbourg geese. In fact, Umbria is probably the world's leading supplier of truffles.

They are just as prolific on Umbrian tables, where they appear with amazing lavishness. My cousins in Piemonte carefully shave theirs, whereas Giuliana slices hers into generous pieces. Here they are pounded with a pestle to make a paste that is heavenly spread on oven-toasted country bread with a squeeze of lemon and a couple of drops of red wine vinegar. Or they use them by the handful, together with olive oil, garlic and anchovies, to make Umbria's most famous spaghetti sauce. This can turn out divine or a disappointment, as just a little too much of these other ingredients can infringe on the the flavor of the truffles. Carefully prepared it is a simple and effective way to elevate any menu and in my family it is a traditional way to see the New Year in. In Alba they ceremoniously shave truffles over eggs fried in butter, whereas in

First, however, there is a lot of work to be done. After making salami such as the *finocchiona* flavored with wild fennel, the *norcino* stuffs the *mazzafegati* (liver sausage seasoned with garlic, pepper and coriander). All the while the pig's head has been boiling and next *soppressata* (headcheese), will be made.

Meanwhile there are several tasty titbits to be tried. The *tegamata* is a classic at this feast. These are the sweetbreads sautéed in olive oil, seasoned with fennel and sampled preferably right out of the pan (*tegame* in Italian). Perfect for an *aperitivo* while waiting for Annetta's *arista* (the roast pork loin) are *ciccioli* (cubes of lard fried in olive oil and wrung out in a cloth so that only the crunchy fibers remain). This is also the traditional time to taste Piero's new wine and Rosa and Lina, who have come to give a hand to Annetta, have brought baskets of their homemade bread that is grilled and eaten anointed liberally with the season's freshly pressed olive oil.

After lunch there is still the *guancia* (pig's cheek) to be rolled and peppered, *fegatelli* to be wrapped (liver encased in the stomach lining) and the *burista* (blood sausage) to be finished. I always look forward to the moment for *sanguinaccio*, sometimes called *frittata nera* (black fritters), a kind of sweet crêpe made with pig's blood fried with crushed almond cookies and olive oil. From the neighboring village of Todi Giuliana has brought back a sampling of the various sweets for which it is famous. One of these, in particular, is admirably suited to this rather primeval feast, an almond cake formed like a serpent with the grotesque head of a gargoyle. These we wash down with La Canonica's velvety Vin Santo and at the conclusion of the day, a glass of Piero's penetrating Grappa assists our digestion.

One goes away from a *festa* such as this wanting to hibernate for the rest of the winter. Even in my comatose state, however, it does occur to me that the next best thing to living in Umbria is to have Giuliana and Piero Dorazio there as neighbors.

For at least six months of the year lunch is taken outside in the garden, on a massive stone table

Norcia they chop them to fill a *frittata*. (The trick with this dish is to cook the eggs but not the truffles.) For a late-night snack you can even order a truffle pizza with a double portion of pecorino cheese. At La Canonica truffles also go into the soup, with tongue and tagliatelle added.

The dramatic climax to Umbria's seasonal culinary cycle is the annual pig-sticking. This region's pork products, especially those that come from Norcia, are renowned throughout Italy. In Roma a pork butcher is called a *norcino*. Shortly after the feast of the Epiphany, when the Christmas crib (which originated here) has been packed away for another year, a local *norcino* comes to La Canonica to slaughter the porker that they have been fattening just for the occasion. The Sunday following, after the meat has hung for a couple of days, he will return for this ancient ritual.

The Dorazio invite their friends and the *festa* begins early in the morning and lasts for almost ten hours. By the time the *norcino* arrives with his impressive array of knives and portable sausage maker, Annetta has already got a good fire going and the sacrificial victim has been laid out on the kitchen table. Before the day is over all two hundred and fifty pounds or more of flesh will have been disposed of in one way or another – cured into prosciutto and pancetta, stuffed into salami and sausages, and the prime cuts cooked and eaten during the course of the *festa*.

While the *norcino* is rubbing the hefty thigh of the porker with a paste of pounded garlic before covering it with salt (after a couple of weeks under salt the prosciutto will be washed and hung in La Canonica's airing room for about eight months), Giuliana has already thrown the ribs and chops on the grill for a mid-morning snack and Annetta has seasoned the loin with fennel in preparation for lunch.

A FAIR WEATHER MENU

MINESTRA DI TARTUFI NERI
Black truffle soup

FRITTATA DI ASPARAGINA
Asparagus omelet

SERPENTE DI TODI
Todi serpent tart

This soup can be made any time of the year using preserved truffles, which are astonishingly flavorful. If truffles cannot be found, button mushrooms cut into julienne strips may be substituted. After this rich start to the meal, the light *frittata* is a perfect second course. It is also a useful dish for brunch or for eating cold on a picnic. Should it not be a good day for baking, hard almond *biscotti*, popular in Umbria as well as Toscana, dipped in an aromatic Umbrian Vin Santo, make a lovely conclusion to this easy yet elegant meal.

Suggested Wines Serve a fruity Orvieto classico with the first two courses and a velvety Vin Santo with dessert.

MINESTRA DI TARTUFI NERI
Black truffle soup

4 oz/125 g cooked veal tongue
1 black truffle

3 1/2 oz/2/3 cup/100 g plain (all-purpose) flour
1 egg
60 fl oz/7 1/2 cups/1.7 liters meat broth (page 189)
salt and pepper

Cut the tongue and truffle into julienne strips.

Make a dough with the flour and egg (as explained on page 188) and roll into a thin sheet. Cut into tagliatelle and leave to dry.

Boil the broth, add the tagliatelle and cook until *al dente*. Add the tongue and truffle, season and remove from the heat and serve.

FRITTATA DI ASPARAGINA
Asparagus omelet

1 1/4 lb/500 g wild asparagus (or small green asparagus)
6 eggs
salt and pepper
3 tbsp grated Parmesan cheese
4 tbsp extra virgin olive oil

Clean the asparagus and blanch briefly in a large pan of boiling salted water. Drain, refresh under cold running water and trim away the hard ends. Beat the eggs in a bowl. Add salt and pepper, the grated cheese and lastly the asparagus.

Heat the oil in a frying pan and add the eggs. Cook over low heat, loosening the bottom gently with a wooden spoon, until the eggs have set. Turn the omelet over onto a dish and then slide it back into the pan. Cook for another couple of minutes until this side has set. Slide onto a platter and serve.

Frittata di asparagina

SERPENTE DI TODI
Todi serpent tart

18 oz/4½ cups/500 g ground almonds
15 oz/2¼ cups/450 g granulated sugar
5-6 egg whites
½ oz/1 tbsp/10 g butter
½ tbsp plain (all-purpose) flour
2 candied cherries
1 tbsp icing (confectioners') sugar

Put all ingredients except the cherries and icing sugar into a bowl. Mix together and work into a smooth dough. Form the dough into the shape of a snake, making the head of larger proportion than the body. Use the cherries for eyes and make scalelike designs on the body with scissor tips.

Place on a buttered and floured baking sheet and cook in the oven at 300°F/160°C/Mark 2 for 40 minutes. Allow to cool, sprinkle with icing sugar and serve.

Serpente di Todi

A WARM WEATHER MENU

SPAGHETTI ALLE OLIVE
Spaghetti with black olives and orange

PETTI DI POLLO RIPIENI
Stuffed chicken breasts

LENTICCHIE IN UMIDO
Stewed lentils

FRUTTA FRESCA
Fresh fruit

Olive sauce with spaghetti is classic. I have added orange, not just for color but because these two flavors combine so well. The olive in the chicken breasts continues this Mediterranean theme but with a different variation.

In Italy we use brown lentils. Until quite recently they were the only ones available and I still find them the most flavorful.

Suggested Wines   Serve a light red wine. The ones that come from the area surrounding Umbria's Lake Trasimeno are flowery and fruity.

SPAGHETTI ALLE OLIVE
Spaghetti with black olives and orange

peel of 2 oranges
1 onion
8 tbsp extra virgin olive oil
3½ oz/⅔ cup/100 g stoned (pitted) black olives
salt and pepper
1¼ lb/600 g spaghetti

Cut the orange peel into julienne strips, then boil in water for 2 minutes.

Chop the onion, and stir-fry in half the olive oil until transparent. Add the olives and orange peel and remove from heat. At the same time,

Spaghetti alle olive

bring to the boil a large pan of salted water and cook the spaghetti until *al dente*. Drain, add the olive mixture, the remaining olive oil, season and serve.

PETTI DI POLLO RIPIENI
Stuffed chicken breasts

2 whole (4 halves) boneless chicken breasts
10 oz/1⅓ cups/300 g olive paste
1 tbsp flour
1 oz/2 tbsp/25 g butter
1 tbsp extra virgin olive oil
½ glass white wine
salt
1 glass milk

Pound the chicken breasts flat. Spread with olive paste, roll up and tie tightly. Dust with flour.

In a frying pan, heat the butter and oil, add the chicken and cook until it colors evenly. Deglaze the pan with the wine. Add salt, cover and cook for about 30 minutes over low heat, adding a little milk whenever necessary. Slice, arrange on a platter and serve.

LENTICCHIE IN UMIDO
Stewed lentils

10 oz/1½ cups/300 g brown lentils
1 slice onion
1 celery stalk
2 oz/50 g pancetta
2 tbsp extra virgin olive oil
1 glass red wine
1 tsp fennel seeds
salt and pepper

Soak the lentils overnight in cold water. Drain.

Finely chop the onion, celery and pancetta, and sauté in a saucepan with the olive oil until transparent. Add the lentils, red wine, fennel seeds, salt and pepper. Cover and cook over low heat for about 30 minutes before serving.

A COLD WEATHER MENU

TORTA DI FUNGHI
Mushroom pie

PALOMBE ALLA GHIOTTA
Wild pigeons stewed in red wine

SPINACI ALL'AGLIO
Spinach sautéed in garlic

PANNA COTTA CON SALSA DI PERE
Cooked cream with pear sauce

I am told that certain parts of both the American and English countryside are full of edible mushrooms waiting to be picked, so there should be no reason for not using fresh ones in season. If necessary, however, champignons can be used as a substitute. In that case, add several dry porcini for flavor.

Guinea fowl and the American rock cornish game hens are also delicious stewed *alla ghiotta*. When I boil spinach I leave the stems on. They cook in the same time as the leaves and are just as tender.

Suggested Wines   This is a menu for "important" wines, both a white and red from Torgiano; a Rubesco riserva would be ideal with the pigeon. Umbria exports a fine dessert wine called Sagrantino di Montefalco, delicious with the cooked cream.

TORTA DI FUNGHI
Mushroom pie

1¼ lb/600 g fresh porcini mushrooms
2 tbsp extra virgin olive oil
5 oz/⅔ cup/150 g butter
9 oz/scant 2 cups/250 g plain (all-purpose) flour
1 egg
salt and pepper
2 tbsp chopped parsley

Clean the mushrooms with a cloth (do not wash them). Slice, then sauté in a frying pan over medium heat in the olive oil and 1 oz/2tbsp/25 g of the butter.

Make a short pastry dough with the flour, the rest of the butter, the egg and salt (as explained on page 00). Knead until smooth. Roll out into a thin sheet and line a 9 in/23 cm pie mold. Cover with a sheet of parchment (silicon) paper and fill with dried beans.

Bake in the oven at 375°F/190°C/Mark 5 for 20 minutes. Remove the beans and continue to bake for another 20 minutes. Unmold, fill with the hot mushrooms, sprinkle with parsley and serve.

PALOMBE ALLA GHIOTTA
Wild pigeons stewed in red wine

3 wild pigeons
35 fl oz/4⅓ cups/ 1 liter red wine
4 fl oz/½ cup/100 ml vinegar
4 cloves garlic
1 sprig rosemary
1 small bunch fresh sage, tied together
1 small onion
3 oz/100 g prosciutto
4 tbsp extra virgin olive oil
4 anchovy fillets in oil
1 tbsp capers in vinegar, rinsed
1 lemon wedge
1 thin slice bread
salt and pepper

Clean the pigeons, leaving heads and feet on, if still attached. Place in a flameproof casserole with all the other ingredients and cook over low heat for about 1½ hours. Then take the pigeons from the casserole, remove and discard heads and feet, if necessary. Halve the pigeons lengthwise and reserve. Continue to heat the sauce for about another hour until it thickens. Remove the rosemary and sage and purée the sauce in a food mill or processor.

Return pigeon halves to the casserole with the sauce, reheat for 10 minutes and serve.

SPINACI ALL'AGLIO
Spinach sautéed in garlic

2¼ lb/1 kg fresh spinach
6 cloves garlic
4 tbsp extra virgin olive oil
salt and pepper

Clean the spinach and cook in a little salted boiling water for a couple of minutes. Drain and squeeze dry.

Sauté the garlic cloves in oil. Add the spinach and sauté for a couple of minutes. Remove the garlic, season with salt and pepper and serve.

PANNA COTTA CON SALSA DI PERE
Cooked cream with pear sauce

16 fl oz/2 cups/450 ml whipping cream
1 cinnamon stick
peel of lemon
4 tbsp sugar
2 tbsp powdered (unflavored) gelatine
For the sauce:
1 tbsp sugar
4 ripe pears

Heat half the cream with the cinnamon, lemon peel and 3 tbsp of the sugar until it reaches the boiling point. Discard the cinnamon and lemon. Soften the gelatine in the cream, mix well and leave to cool completely. Whip the remaining cream with remaining sugar until stiff, and fold gently into the chilled cream.

Wet 6 individual molds, fill with the chilled cream and leave to set in refrigerator for at least 2 hours.

To make the sauce, boil the sugar with 2 tbsp of water for 1 minute. Peel and slice the pears. Purée with a food mill or processor together with the sugar syrup until velvety. Unmold the cream and serve surrounded with the pear sauce.

Palombe alla ghiotta

Torta di funghi

LAZIO

PALAZZO TAVERNA A ROMA

Fabulous food in the palace of Princess Stefanina Aldobrandini

"Once upon a time there was a beautiful, young princess who lived in a grand and splendid palace. But its magnificent drawing rooms with their marble floors and ornate ceilings were dark and dreary because all the windows had been shuttered. So the princess said, 'I shall give a great banquet and invite hundreds of people.' She ordered her chef to prepare immense platters of food and the servants to lay the tables with satin cloths, crystal and silver. Guests came from every part of the world. They feasted on her fine food and drink and enjoyed themselves so much that they kept coming back. So the princess decided to put on banquets all over the kingdom where they are now an enormous success and she lives happily ever after."

Like all fairy tales, this one is a mixture of fantasy and reality. The beautiful young princess is real – Princess Stefanina Aldobrandini –

The basilica of San Pietro and the Via della Conciliazione, Roma,
and above the sitting room of Palazzo Taverna

and her palace really exists, the superb Palazzo Taverna in the heart of Renaissance Roma. She and her sisters were born and raised in its magnificent rooms but when the family grew up and left home (Stefanina married Prince Clemente Aldobrandini and with their three children live nearby) her mother, March-esa Lavinia Taverna Gallarati-Scotti moved upstairs to smaller, sunnier rooms with magnificent views of Roma. The grand drawing rooms were only opened on special occasions and a few times even used as a film set.

Several years ago Stefanina really did decide to throw open the shutters of Palazzo Taverna and use its splendid rooms for banquets. She found a ready clientele especially in the numerous national and international concerns with representation in the capital who were searching for just such a sumptuous ambiance in which to entertain. Now her palace glitters and glows with cocktail and dinner parties, large and small, festive family occasions, receptions and balls. She has expanded her business to include a catering service, a relatively new idea in Italy, and organizes the food for prestigious events all over the country. Recently she opened a shop in Roma where customers can take away some of her fabulous dishes, and a country restaurant outside the city. She personally directs the entire activity, including menu, food preparation, decorations and service and her personality and presence can be felt in every detail.

Stefanina has initiated a renaissance of Italian cooking and entertaining that represents a particularly Roman tradition of gastronomy. After all, the very name of the Roman general, Lucullus, is synonymous with lavish banquets and although Epicurus was a Greek, it was his Roman disciples who brough epicureanism to its most refined expression. And quite apart from stuffed bear, peacock pâté, marinated parrot's tongue and all the other exotic extravaganzas of imperial feasts, the Romans did develop the first European cuisine in the cultural sense. The first attempt to document

Piazza Navona and Bernini's famous statues

the ingredients and procedures for preparing certain kinds of food was made by Apicius in the First Century and the manuscript recording his research must be considered the forerunner of all recipe books that were to follow. Although much of what he recorded is bizarre, he also handed down to posterity the exquisite idea of combining figs and melon and of baking kid in wine and honey, both popular dishes with his countrymen today.

The Barbarian invasions of Roma were but a brief, dark interval in the epicurean history of that civilization. Already by the High Middle Ages, Dante, in *La Divina Commedia*, has put poor Pope Nicolas IV, a Frenchman, in purgatory sweating off his sins of gluttony. It seems his Holiness was inordinately fond of drowning live eels from the nearby lake of Bolsena in Vernaccia wine at the table before sending them to the kitchen to be fried for his pleasure. These same eels, *capitoni*, bought live (but not done in at the table,) marinated in

white wine and grilled, seasoned with bay, are still considered a Roman Christmas delicacy.

The first printed book on gastronomy was also written in Roma, by Bartolomeo Sacchi, who is usually referred to as Platina, at the beginning of the Renaissance. One of his lasting contributions was to advise putting some rational and digestive order to a meal. He counsels beginning with light foods, such as greens, fruit, vegetables cooked and raw, and eggs, and proceeding from there. As we shall see, these types of antipasto are an important first course to a modern Roman meal.

During the High Renaissance not only did popes and princes vie with each other for the best cooks, they commissioned the finest artisans and artists of their day to create beautiful settings for their feasts. Benvenuto Cellini fashioned his famous golden saltcellar and Leonardo da Vinci designed banquet sets. By the seventeenth and eighteenth centuries *trionfi da tavola*, "triumphs of the table," flamboyant sculptures of the food itself, predecessors of our centerpieces, often seemed to have assumed more importance at the banquet than the food itself. Their influence can be seen in the fanciful displays, especially of fish, in the windows of many Roman restaurants.

What all those centuries of Roman gastronomic tradition have contributed of enduring value to our ways of cooking and eating is an enlargement of our imagination with the possibility of transforming a meal into a festive banquet. This is still a very characteristic Roman approach to food and it is an ability that crosses all social and economic boundaries. You feel this immediately when eating out in Roma. It is especially indicative that all Romans adore to eat in public, preferably in their streets and piazzas. Whether in a simple *osteria* or an elegant restaurant there is an atmosphere of conviviality and a sensuality in how the food is prepared, presented and enjoyed that makes one feel part of a very ancient and civilized tradition.

The festive feeling begins long before the meal in the many open food markets scattered throughout the city, perhaps another legacy of Imperial Rome. The quality and quantity of the produce, the way in which it is displayed and the earthy zest of the vendors create the mood. Then there are the numerous small stores and tiny indoor stalls that have survived in some of the older neighborhoods. I remember one under the apartment where my daughter used to live in Roma. The old monger, a real character, sold his few fresh fish well before noon and spent the rest of the day sitting at the entrance to his stall listening, at high volume, to old opera recordings.

The real feast begins with the gorgeous and abundant arrangement of antipasti that greet you as you enter the dining room. It was the custom in Roma, at least from Renaissance times, to begin a banquet with a series of cold dishes served on a sideboard and seasoned with both sweet and savory sauces. The tradition flourishes. Sometimes you are even served an

The dining room, Palazzo Taverna

ante-antipasto, just to get you in the spirit of things, usually warm *suppli' alla romana*, rice croquettes filled with a mixture of meats, cheese and mushrooms. The choice on the

platters is tantalizing: *crostini alla provatura e alici*, little toasts with pieces of melted provatura, an egg-shaped buffalo cheese from Lazio, with a sauce of anchovies cooked in butter; *carciofi alla romana*, little artichokes stripped to their tenderest parts, stuffed with garlic and mint and cooked in olive oil; *cipolline in agro dolce*, tiny, new onions, flavored with bay and cloves and simmered in sugar and vinegar; a colorful arrangement of sliced eggs, roasted red, yellow and green peppers and juicy tomatoes seasoned with anchovy fillets, parsley and basil; dishes of various shellfish, especially mussels and *ricci*, sea-urchins. Romans are particularly fond of tuna as an antipasto. Chunks of it are commonly mixed with white beans and also with artichoke hearts. At a banquet I attended in Palazzo Taverna for an international awards ceremony, Stefanina served it in the form of a light and elegant *spuma di tonno*, literally a "froth of tuna," a kind of mousse of tuna and puréed potatoes molded in a ring.

Roman family cooking, in particular, has an ancient tradition of preparing soups, from light broths to dense concoctions with whole wheat and vegetables. These last are all the descendants of the ancient Roman *pultes*, a kind of porridge that was a staple in the diet of the military on the march (as well as the traditional dish for the wedding night!). The nearest of kin on the menu today is *farricello con le cotiche*, made with a very fine flour from spelt, cooked with pork rind and seasoned with garlic, marjoram, onion, tomato, parsley and basil. Potions of broth seem to have been popular for aiding the digestion in between the endless courses of a classical banquet. The best known modern version of this kind of soup is *stracciatella*, made from chicken broth with some egg, flour, grated pecorino cheese and a little lemon peel beaten in. Princess Aldobrandini often begins a formal supper with a similar broth called *passatelli in brodo*. Here a paste of breadcrumbs and Parmesan cheese is "passed" through a special type of sieve in order to form short, spaghetti-like pieces that are added to the boiling consommé.

When it comes to *pastasciutta*, truly all roads lead to Roma. Semolina gnocchi and spaghetti are perhaps the most common, whereas the most typically Roman – probably going back to Cicero's beloved *laganum* – are *fettuccine*, strips of dough boiled in water. These are long, thin, fresh egg noodles, classically seasoned simply with a double or even triple portion of butter and a generous amount of grated cheese while they are still steaming hot. On the menus of Palazzo Taverna, a banquet alternative to pasta, which is virtually impossible for a large number of guests, is a handsome and delicious *crostata di formaggio*, a rich crusty pie seasoned with three cheeses.

Magnificent door handle

Of all the Italian regional capitals, Roma has the finest tradition of fish dishes. Their variety and the repertoire of recipes is really astonishing. This must be due primarily to a taste preference, because there are other cities with an even larger supply closer at hand. Romans make wide use of crustaceans and molluscs both as antipasti and with pasta. In the eating establishments of Trastevere, especially, you will see proud displays of every kind of fish the Mediterranean has to offer, waiting to be grilled or steamed with a variety of fresh herbs. At a dinner party at Palazzo Taverna you might expect to have *triglia*, a highly prized variety of red mullet, brought whole to your table by a waiter wearing white coat and gloves. After he serves your portion, you will find it has been stuffed with wild fennel, beautifully wrapped in prosciutto and perfectly cooked in white wine and lemon juice.

The most ancient aristocrat among the region's rare meat dishes is the venerated *abbacchio*, eulogized by the Latin poet, Juvenal, in a celebrated stanza, which loosely translated could be rendered, "the tenderest of the flock, with more milk than blood, that has not lost its virginity by eating grass." Tradition dictates that it should be not less than thirty days old nor more than sixty. Any younger, it would still have too much baby fat; any older it would have lost much of its "virginal" tenderness. In its most classical form it is roasted with garlic and rosemary together with a few potatoes. Its tiny chops, greased with lard and eaten right off the grill, *a scottadito* (so they burn your fingers) is a perfect picnic dish. For her banquets Stefanina would rather roast a fine cut of veal, not a typically Roman meat but more practical and refined. The flavor of Roma is added in the sauce of anchovies, a favorite Roman culinary component reminiscent of the ancient imperial condiment, *garum*, that was apparently a kind of anchovy paste.

When I think of the greens and vegetables of Roma, I immediately have visions of its glorious salads. There may be other regions that grow larger quantities and have even more variety but once again it is the Romans who know how to make every dish festive. I find it irritating and frustrating to order a salad in other places in Italy and have an uninspiring plate of *lattuga*, common lettuce, put before me, especially when I had seen perfectly wonderful greens in their market that very morning. In Roma's Campo dei Fiori marvelous old women spend the mornings washing and picking through bushels of little greens preparing *misticanza* for their customers, who include many of the city's best restaurants. This is an aromatic and flavorful mixture of herbs and little lettuces, cultivated and wild. On any one day it might include (and I will

Piazza di Spagna and flower-covered steps to the Trinità dei Monti

give them their melodic Roman names,) *acetosa, barba di frate, bucalossi, caccialepre, cicorietta, erbanoce, crespigno, indiviola, lattughella, ojosa, piededipapavero, piedigallo, radiciotte* and *raponzoli* and at least several others.

As an accompaniment to his impressive stuffed pheasant, the chef at Palazzo Taverna uses Roma's abundant vegetables to advantage by decorating the platter with little mounds of a variety of colorful braised carrots, beets, green beans, corn and tiny onions. An unusual looking and delicious tasting vegetable that has recently arrived on the Roman market stalls is *sedano rapa* (celeriac.) The bulbs are sweet and juicy and I have enjoyed it at a banquet catered by Stefanina with a creamy cheese sauce served in a mold.

Romans prefer to finish their meals with fresh fruit, and a slice of watermelon to end an *al fresco* feast in the summertime is a great favorite – it is also sold from stalls all over the city. At Palazzo Taverna this typical flavor is presented as a dessert gelatine with bitter chocolate drops.

If you choose to conclude more ambitiously with a pastry, you will often find it filled with the local ricotta cheese. An easy and elegant way to capture the savor of a Roman banquet is to end your own feast with Princess Stefanina's recipe for a delicious ricotta dessert enriched with whipping cream, flavored with coffee and brandy and served, of course, in crystal goblets.

MENU FOR A LUCULLIAN BANQUET

SPUMA DI TONNO
Tuna mousse

FAGIANO FARCITO
Stuffed pheasant

VERDURE STUFATE
Braised vegetables

COPPE DI RICOTTA AL CAFFÈ
Ricotta dessert with coffee

This elegant mousse can be made without the gelatine and prepared in just a few minutes. I sometimes serve it as the main course for luncheon.

Boning pheasant is a painstaking process. An alternative is to stuff it whole, in which case the ingredients should be reduced by a quarter.

In Lazio, as in Toscana, ricotta cheese is traditionally made from sheep's milk. It is more flavorful than cow's milk ricotta, but either can be used for this simple and rich dessert.

Suggested Wines With these three simplified but still sumptuous menus only the region's best should be served. Most of Lazio's wines are white. Besides the well known Frascati from the Castelli Romani there is elegant Fiorano Bianco and the fruity Marino. The finest reds are Colle Picchioni and Fiorano Rosso, which is made from Merlot and Cabernet Sauvignon.

Spuma di tonno

SPUMA DI TONNO
Tuna mousse

3 tbsp powdered (unflavored) gelatine
16 fl oz/2 cups/450 ml beef broth (page 189)
1 egg plus 2 yolks
10 fl oz/1¼ cups/300 ml extra virgin olive oil
1 lb/500 g tuna in olive oil
juice of 1 lemon
4 large potatoes

Prepare the gelatine by dissolving half the powder in the broth. Pour onto a plate and refrigerate for at least 3 hours. Chop finely.

Make a mayonnaise in a processor with the egg and the yolks, adding the oil in a steady stream. Add a pinch of salt and finally ¼ of the tuna.

Heat the lemon juice and use it to dissolve the rest of the gelatine. Leave to cool, then add to the mayonnaise.

Boil the potatoes and pass through a food mill or food processor while still hot. Pass the remaining tuna through a mill, then mix with the potatoes and 3 tbsp mayonnaise. Pour the mixture into an oiled ring mold, pack down well, smooth the surface and unmold onto a serving platter.

Cover completely with the rest of the mayonnaise and smooth the surface with the blade of a knife dipped in cold water. Refrigerate for several hours, surround with the chopped gelatine and serve.

FAGIANO FARCITO
Stuffed pheasant

1 handful dried porcini mushrooms
1 handful raisins
3½ oz/100 g lean pork
3½ oz/100 g lean beef
7 oz/200 g ham
3½ oz/100 g pancetta
1 sprig rosemary
3½ oz/scant 1 cup/100 g grated Parmesan cheese
1 handful pine nuts
1 egg
small glass of brandy
pinch of grated nutmeg
1 black truffle (optional)
1 large pheasant
1 oz/2 tbsp/25 g butter
2 tbsp extra virgin olive oil
1 glass dry white wine
salt and pepper

Soak the mushrooms and raisins separately in water for about 30 minutes. Finely chop the pork, beef, ham, pancetta, mushrooms and rosemary. Combine in a bowl with the Parmesan, raisins, pine nuts, egg, brandy and nutmeg and mix well. Add sliced truffle if desired.

Bone the pheasant and stuff with the mixture, beginning with the thighs and filling out its form. Truss and tie well. Place in a casserole with the butter and oil and cook in the oven at 350°F/180°C/Mark 4 for about 1½ hours. During the last 30 minutes baste with the wine, adding a little at a time, scraping up the cooking juices from the base of the casserole. Place the pheasant on a platter, strain the cooking juices and serve them separately.

VERDURE STUFATE
Braised vegetables

7 oz/200 g carrots
1 large beetroot (beet)
7 oz/200 g green beans
7 oz/1 cup/200 g fresh corn kernels
5 tbsp extra virgin olive oil
7 oz/200 g baby onions
½ glass red wine vinegar
1 tbsp sugar
salt

Cook each vegetable (except onions) separately

Fagiano farcito e verdure stufate

in a large pan of boiling, salted water, then drain. Slice the carrot and cut the beetroot (beet) into strips. Put the carrots, beetroot, green beans and corn into 4 separate saucepans, each with 1 tbsp oil. Cook for about 10 minutes over low heat, stirring occasionally.

Place the onions in another saucepan, add the rest of the oil, the vinegar, sugar and salt and cook for about 20 minutes over low heat.

Place the vegetables around the pheasant on the platter and serve.

COPPE DI RICOTTA AL CAFFÈ
Ricotta dessert with coffee

8 fl oz/1 cup/225 ml whipping cream
1 lb/450 g ricotta
1 glass brandy
4 tbsp ground espresso coffee
4 oz/¹/₂ cup/125 g sugar
1 handful coffee grains

Beat the whipping cream until firm. Blend together the ricotta, brandy and ground coffee with the sugar. Fold in the cream gently, put the mixture into 6 crystal goblets, decorate with the coffee grains and serve.

MENU FOR A SABINE SUPPER

PASSATELLI IN BRODO
Chicken broth with Parmesan and breadcrumbs

*SFORMATO DI SEDANO RAPA
ALLA CREMA*
Celeriac mold with cream cheese

TRIGLIE AL PROSCIUTTO
Red mullet with fennel and prosciutto

BOMBA DI ARANCE
Orange rice mold

The *passatelli* should come out like little worms and, comparisons aside, this dish makes a light and refined first course. The broth can be enriched with very finely chopped ham.

Genuine fontina comes from Valle d'Aosta in the North of Italy but fontina-type cheeses are produced in other regions. It should be delicately sweet and slightly nutty and in this *sformato* can be replaced with any semi-firm, flavorful cheese. Broccoli works well as an alternative to celeriac in this recipe and trout for red mullet. Boiled potatoes served simply with chopped parsley could accompany the fish.

In the North, rice is used as a first course, but in the South, it is frequently prepared as a dessert. Use blood oranges if possible in this mold.

PASSATELLI IN BRODO
Chicken broth with Parmesan and breadcrumbs

5 oz/1 1/4 cups/150 g grated Parmesan cheese
4 oz/1 cup/125 g dried breadcrumbs
peel of 1 lemon
3 eggs
pinch of grated nutmeg
pepper
50 fl oz/6 1/4 cups/1.4 liters chicken broth (page 189)

Mix together all the ingredients except the broth to form a medium soft dough. Put the mixture through a food mill using the largest holes available. Boil the broth, add the paste and cook until it comes to the boil again. Serve immediately.

SFORMATO DI SEDANO RAPA
ALLA CREMA
Celeriac mold with cream cheese

2 1/4 lb/1 kg celeriac or broccoli
2 oz/4 tbsp/50 g butter
salt and pepper
8 fl oz/1 cup/225 ml whipping cream
4 eggs
7 oz/200 g fontina cheese
1 glass white wine
1 tbsp chopped parsley

Peel and slice the celeriac or prepare the broccoli. Cook in a covered saucepan over very low heat with the butter and salt.

Purée through a food mill or food processor, add half the cream and all the eggs, and mix well. Pour the mixture into a buttered and floured mold, place in a larger pan of water and cook in the oven at 350°F/180°C/Mark 4 for about 1 hour.

Cut the fontina into pieces and melt it over low heat, together with the white wine and remaining cream, stirring continuously.

Unmold onto a platter, pour the cream cheese into the center, sprinkle with parsley and serve.

TRIGLIE AL PROSCIUTTO
Red mullet with fennel and prosciutto

6 red mullet
salt and pepper
6 bunches wild fennel, or pieces of bulb fennel
6 slices prosciutto
3 tbsp extra virgin olive oil
1/2 glass white wine
juice of 1/2 lemon

Clean the mullet and stuff with the fennel. Add salt and pepper and wrap each one in a slice of prosciutto.

Oil a frying pan large enough to hold the mullet, put them in together with the rest of the olive oil, the white wine and lemon juice. Cover and cook over low heat for about 15 minutes. If at the end of cooking there is still a lot of liquid, remove the mullet to a platter, reduce the liquid over moderate heat, pour over the mullet and serve.

BOMBA DI ARANCE
Orange rice mold

7 oz/1 cup/200 g rice
salt
16 fl oz/2 cups/450 ml milk
6 egg yolks
6 oranges
7 oz/1 3/4 cups/200 g shelled walnuts
8 oz/1 cup/225 g sugar
3 1/2 oz/7 tbsp/100 g butter
8 fl oz/1 cup/225 ml whipping cream

Boil the rice in a saucepan of lightly salted water for 5 minutes. Drain and cook over low heat with the milk, stirring frequently, until the milk is absorbed and the rice is reduced to a thick cream. Leave to cool.

Add the egg yolks, juice and grated peel of 4 oranges, half the walnuts, sugar, butter and half the cream. Pour into a buttered mold and place in a pan of water in the oven and cook at 350°F/180°C/Mark 4 for about 60 minutes.

Unmold on a serving platter and leave to cool. Beat the rest of the cream until firm and spread over the orange mold. Refrigerate for several hours, decorate with slices of the remaining oranges and walnuts and serve.

Bomba di arance
Sformato di sedano rapa alla crema

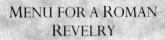

MENU FOR A ROMAN REVELRY

CROSTATA DI FORMAGGIO
Cheese pie

ARROSTO ALLE ACCIUGHE
Veal roasted in anchovy sauce

ZUCCHINE ALLA MENTA
Fried courgettes (zucchini) with mint

GELATINA D'ANGURIA
Watermelon gelatine

When I tested this *crostata*, I tried the leftovers cold the next day and they were excellent. For the veal dish, choose a cut that will not dry out in the lengthy roasting. Good red wine should also be used; cheap wine would give the sauce an acid taste. Briefly blanched, diced fennel and artichokes can be prepared in the same way as the courgettes (zucchini), and honeydew melon is a good alternative to watermelon for the gelatine dessert.

CROSTATA DI FORMAGGIO
Cheese pie

10 oz/2 cups/300 g plain (all-purpose) flour
salt and pepper
4 eggs plus 2 yolks
5 oz/10 tbsp/150 g butter
12 oz/350 g fontina cheese
3½ oz/scant 1 cup/100 g grated Parmesan cheese
3½ oz/100 g gorgonzola cheese
pinch of grated nutmeg
4 fl oz/½ cup/125 ml whipping cream
½ glass white wine
1 black truffle (optional)

Heap the flour in a mound on the working surface. Make a well in the center and add a pinch of salt, the 2 egg yolks and the softened butter and make a short pastry dough (as explained on page 188). Roll out and line a buttered and floured 8-9 in/20-22 cm spring-clip (springform) pan.

Reserve 2 oz/50 g of fontina and grate the rest. Put into a bowl and blend in the Parmesan and gorgonzola using a fork. Add the nutmeg, cream and white wine and mix well. Beat the eggs, add pepper and blend with the cheeses. Fill the pastry shell.

Bake in the oven at 350°F/180°C/Mark 4 for about 45 minutes. Arrange on a platter, cover with julienne strips of the remaining fontina and of the truffle and serve.

ARROSTO ALLE ACCIUGHE
Veal roasted in anchovy sauce

1 oz/25 g dried porcini mushrooms
2 lb/1 kg veal, suitable for roasting
1 handful fresh sage
2 sprigs rosemary
1 oz/2 tbsp/25 g butter
1 tbsp extra virgin olive oil
18 fl oz/2 cups/500 ml red wine
½ onion
4 anchovy fillets in oil
salt

Soak the mushrooms in water for 30 minutes. Squeeze dry. Strain the water and reserve.

Top the veal with the sage leaves and rosemary and tie well. Place in a roasting pan with the butter and oil and cook in the oven at 350°F/180°C/Mark 4 for about 1½ hours.

Meanwhile, chop the onion and fry over low heat together with the mushrooms, wine and anchovy fillets, until the liquid is reduced to half a glass. Purée in a food processor, season and reheat. Pour this sauce over the veal and add reserved mushroom water, scraping the sediment off the roasting pan. Cover and continue to cook for 10 minutes, turning the meat once. Remove the meat, untie, discard the rosemary and sage, cut into slices and arrange on a serving platter. Strain the cooking juices directly over the roast and serve.

ZUCCHINE ALLA MENTA
Fried courgettes (zucchini) with mint

6 courgettes (zucchini)
1 egg
salt
2 tbsp plain (all-purpose) flour
4 oz/1 cup/125 g dried breadcrumbs
2 oz/4 tbsp/50 g butter
4 tbsp extra virgin olive oil
3 tbsp white wine vinegar
1 tbsp mint leaves
1 tbsp sugar

Clean and trim the courgettes (zucchini), slice lengthwise, and dry. Beat the egg with a pinch of salt on a plate. Dust the courgettes (zucchini) with flour, dip in the egg, and coat with breadcrumbs.

Heat the butter and oil in a frying pan and fry the vegetables for a couple of minutes on each side until they turn golden. Drain on paper towels. Heat the vinegar with the mint and sugar in a pan. Boil for a couple of seconds. Arrange the courgettes (zucchini) on a dish, pour over the vinegar and serve.

GELATINA D'ANGURIA
Watermelon gelatine

4½ lb/2 kg watermelon
8 oz/1 cup/225 g sugar
3 tbsp powdered (unflavored) gelatine
6 oz/1 cup/180 g plain (semisweet) chocolate bits

Scrape the pulp from the watermelon and discard the seeds. Pass the pulp through a food mill, then cook over low heat with the sugar for about 10 minutes, stirring frequently. Remove from the heat. Dissolve the gelatine in a little warm water, then stir into the mixture. When it has almost completely cooled, add the chocolate bits.

Pour the mixture into 6 individual molds dipped in cold water. Refrigerate for several hours before unmolding to serve.

CAMPANIA

PALAZZO CALABRITTO A NAPOLI

Cooking with Marquess Franco Santasilia di Torpino
and the last of the Monzù

Without any doubt, the Italian regional cooking best known throughout the world, from Frankfurt to Tokyo and now even in Russia via the USA is Neapolitan. Pizza is only the international symbol of the cuisine of Napoli. Almost as world-renowned are its two classical pasta dishes, *spaghetti al pomodoro* (spaghetti with tomato sauce) and *maccheroni al sugo* (macaroni with meat sauce). Mozzarella cheese is practically as popular as Parmesan and the best in the world, made from fresh buffalo milk, comes from the provinces of Caserta and Salerno where herds of buffalo still graze along the coast. Just as Bologna is the culinary capital of the North, Napoli and its region of Campania is the capital of Southern Italian cuisine.

The cooking of Napoli has been so popular-

Sideboard display including portraits of Umberto di Savoia and his wife Maria Josè

following suit. These fashionable – and, one would imagine, temperamental – chefs were respectfully called *Monsieur* even by their lords and ladies, and soon that title was corrupted in Neapolitan dialect to *Monzù*. It was the practice of these Monzù to hire at their own expense assistants from the local work force who were little more than illiterate scullery-boys. The cleverest of these would eventually pick up or be confided with the jealously guarded culinary secrets of the Monzù. After the first generation of French, the Monzù became a Neapolitan institution and by the following century they had developed a cuisine that was a blend of Gallic inspiration, local food products and Neapolitan flair. This new indigenous cuisine came to its height in the nineteenth century and thrived until the Second World War, when family chefs became a luxury few could afford. A number of Monzù went to cook at the private clubs that began to flourish in the city after the war, frequented by many of their ex-employers.

In those changed times and circumstances it did not take long for the culinary tradition these men represented to disappear. It virtually had, until along came a friend of my youth, Franco Santasilia di Torpino, who wrote a

Franco Santasilia's father collected large wooden replicas of sixteenth-century galleons

ized and internationalized that one has to return to the source to remember how really good it is. To those of us, even in Italy, used to tasting mozzarella several days old or made from cow's milk, eating the genuine cheese fresh, when it is not even a day old, can be an unforgettable gastronomic experience. It is a lively white, soft but solid, dripping with its own milk and has a delicate, sweet fragrance and flavor. Even deep-fried in this state, the famous *mozzarella in carrozza* (in a carriage,) it retains all these qualities, and if fried with the proper light touch, will still release some liquid when cut with a fork.

The same holds true of pizza. In its home-town it is superior. I am not so much thinking of the ingredients, although it would be difficult to improve on olive oil, fresh tomato, garlic, oregano or basil, but of the dough itself. Who knows whether this is due to the type of flour, the moisture in the air, the kind of oven, the skill of the *pizzaiolo* or a

combination of all of these? One thing is sure, it cannot be duplicated elsewhere.

In the fullest sense of the word, all this is *popular* Neapolitan cooking – of the people, by the people and for the people and it is as colorful and zesty as they are. No less exuberant but very much less known is the particular cuisine of the region's great noble families. This is a way of cooking that began to take shape in the second half of the eighteenth century when the kingdom of Napoli was ruled by the Bourbon monarchy. Queen Maria Carolina, sister of Marie Antoinette, did an about-face on what Caterina de'Medici had done from Toscana some two hundred and fifty years before. It would seem Her Majesty thought the popular cooking of her kingdom tasty enough but thoroughly unpresentable at court, so she asked her sister to send over a few chefs from Paris to give it some class.

Her experiment was a huge success and she soon had all the noble families of the realm book entitled *La cucina aristocratica napoletana*, in which he not only documents this cooking but encourages its renewal and adaptation. Franco is from an ancient aristocratic family who came to Napoli with the Spanish Bourbons. We met during summer holidays at his cousin's villa in Positano when we were both students. He became an electrical engineer and the last I heard had gone to California to work for a large international corporation. As it happened, it was there he tried his hand at cooking for the first time, as a pastime in a foreign country that would provide him with something familiar to eat. After his return to Italy Franco's interest in cooking grew from a practical hobby to a gastronomic cultural pursuit. In his spare time he tried to re-create some of the dishes he remembered from his youth. This led him to the more ambitious project of the book and the serious research it entailed.

In this task he elicited first of all the memories of his mother, the Marchesa Leopoldina Caracciolo di Castagneto, who belongs to one of Napoli's oldest families. In her long lifetime she has known many Monzù, of her own family and household and those of friends. He also solicited recipes and remembrances from other relatives and friends.

In the kitchen he enlisted the skills of his mother's cook, Gerardo Modugno, a man who merits the title "Last of the Monzù." Gerardo began his career as assistant to the old family chef, Monzù Federico. In those days, he recalls, to be accepted for the job you had to cook to the satisfaction of the Monzù three basic dishes: *spiedini* (skewered meats,) *granatine* (a sort of elegant meat patty) and *fritto misto* (a mixed deep fry.) To this day *fritto misto alla napoletana* is perhaps Gerardo's most acclaimed and requested dish. Apart from the sheer number of foods fried (Gerardo does up to twenty and recalls legendary Monzù who could do over thirty,) it requires perfect timing for they ought literally to come out of the pan and on to the table hot and crispy in sequence of

Palazzo Calabritto and the Piazza dei Martiri

execution. Besides a variety of vegetables, courgette (zucchini) flowers, asparagus tips, tomatoes, peppers, onions, fennel, the traditional Neapolitan deep fry consists of rice balls, *crocchè* of potatoes, *panzerotti* (fritters filled with cheese) and sometimes little meatballs and a choux of tiny fish. Each must be dipped in just the right amount of batter and fried in an order calculated according to the cooking odors the foods emit in the oil.

Together Franco and Gerardo re-created over fifty recipes for the book (the Monzù never confided their secrets to paper.) Some they simplified in time and technique in order to make them more accessible to contemporary cooking, and sometimes they adapted the ingredients, especially fat content, to today's tastes.

Others they transmitted in all their original complexity and grandeur as testimony to the accomplishments of a vanished culture. When I asked Gerardo if I could streamline a few

even more, he agreed somewhat reluctantly, as if I were taking most of the fun out of cooking. He delights in putting his skills to the test and one rather spectacular recipe he thoroughly enjoys is a tricolored *timballo*. This dish, created by Monzù Cesare, chef to Franco's grandfather, Prince Caracciolo, when he was ambassador to Budapest in the 'twenties, was the *pièce de résistance* at the Embassy's annual banquet for foreign delegations on the king's birthday. Its cupola shape is divided on the inside into three sections, each with a different filling of prosciutto, pork and spinach, and on the outside of the dome each section is covered in one of the national colors of Italy: very thin horizontal slices of tomatoes for red, long string beans for green and individual strings of white spaghetti inlaid horizontally. Not a feat for the faint-hearted!

Another dish that gives him much satisfaction comes directly from the court cooks of Maria Carolina and is called *timballo flammand*.

A dome-shaped mold is lined by winding individual strands of thick spaghetti (bucatini) in a spiral effect. This is layered with a complex filling of mushrooms, truffles, veal, chicken, prosciutto, Parmesan, blended with a béchamel and meat sauce and oven-baked in a double boiler. This is perhaps the most elaborate and refined creation of the *cucina aristocratica napoletana* and not many professional cooks, Gerardo comments with justifiable pride, could bring it off.

Not many of the recipes in Franco's book are of similar bravura. Some, as I discovered at the several dinner parties he gave to test them out on fortunate friends, are even simple, although by no means plain. The test of a fine cook is not only mastery of culinary techniques but perhaps more importantly the ability to improvise something appetizing out of nothing. Franco's mother remembered a dish that Monzù Vincenzo Migliardi concocted when Umberto di Savoia, then Prince of Piemonte and later the last King of Italy, paid them an unexpected visit. There was not much in the refrigerator that summer's day but with some canned tuna, an egg and fresh green beans from the corner store, he created a marvelous tuna mousse in a ring mold and to please the Prince, encased it with the beans. Since it is served cold, decorating it with the beans is not a big problem. It just takes time and patience.

The Prince must have enjoyed the meal because he came back, this time with his wife, Princess Maria José. On this occasion Monzù Vincenzo outdid himself, maybe to make up for the canned tuna, with an exquisite meat loaf baked in a crust. The future King and Queen of Italy left behind autographed photos, so they were obviously pleased with the results. Gerardo prepared it for us according to the same recipe, which I have somewhat simplified. It is a beautiful dish to present to your guests and absolutely delicious. And speaking of autographed photos, one of Gerardo's prized memorabilia that he keeps in his kitchen is a photograph with a dedication from the same Umberto, by that time monarch in exile, given him in recognition of his splendid services as cook during a yachting trip on the Mediterranean – the French part, of course!

At the same meal, Franco prepared a salad according to an old recipe from his father's family. It is composed on a bed of mixed endive and red radicchio, with slices of fennel, radishes and cheese added, all covered with pomegranate seeds. Both he and I thought it interesting that its combination of ingredients resembles the many imaginative salads that are served today, especially in the fine restaurants of California.

Do not for a moment think that the Neapolitan aristocracy went without their pizza. In his book Franco gives a family recipe for the ultimate pizza pie and confesses it was the dish he missed most when he left Napoli. It is topped with traditional ingredients, tomato sauce, basil, garlic, olive oil, *mozzarella di bufala* and ham, but the crust is further enriched with egg, milk and butter, kneaded for at least half an hour, and puffs up several inches high. I especially like Franco's simple recipe taken from a friend's early nineteenth-century cookery notebook for tiny sweet and savory pizzas made with sugar and cheese.

Some of the most interesting recipes were given Franco by his cousins, Maurizio and Mirella Barracco. Several years ago they formed a private foundation called Napoli Novantanove (Naples '99) with the scope of

Local oysters

promoting the city's artistic heritage and intellectual tradition and of raising funds to restore its cultural patrimony. Franco views his involvement with the tradition of Neapolitan gastronomy as part of this larger renaissance of Napoli. In 1937, Maurizio's father bought the spectacular Villa Emma, which overlooks the sea at Posillipo and was given by Admiral Nelson to Lady Hamilton. From that veritable paradise comes a recipe for one of the most imaginative and tasty ways to serve pasta. A round of provolone cheese is hollowed out and filled with rigatoni seasoned with a sauce of mushrooms, meat, chicken liver and sausage. Provolone is also used in the sauce and adds its characteristic piquancy. This cheese is another specialty of Campania, although Franco tells me the very best comes from the Sila area of Calabria. It was originally made from buffalo milk but today cow's milk is used instead. It is rich, firm and flavorful, sweet when young and sharp with age. Aged provolone is used in this recipe.

Gerardo not only helped Franco recreate these recipes but passed on several that he had inherited himself. One of these that I particularly enjoy because it is uncomplicated and easy (although it does need a good deal of preparation,) as well as extremely tasty and impressive, is his *sartù di riso*. This mold is one of the few Neapolitan rice dishes. (In the South of Italy rice is more often prepared as a dessert.) It is made with an amazing number of ingredients, twenty-five in Gerardo's original, which I have reduced to twenty. Traditionally *sartù* are rather monumental, tall and thin. Gerardo's comes out in an elegant form of pleasing proportions.

The Southern Italian penchant for all things sweet begins at Napoli. Although competition is tight, there is good evidence to support the claim that Neapolitan ice cream is the best in the world. Neapolitans know how to achieve a subtle balance between a rich creaminess and sharp flavor. They are fond as well of puff pastries filled with another Neapolitan specialty,

Panorama across central Napoli from Castel Sant'Elmo

chocolate. The most classical of all their homemade pastries is *pastiera*, a sweet short pastry dough filled with fresh ricotta cheese and candied fruit. This is the traditional Easter tart of Campania. Members of even the same family have their own rendition and part of the holiday celebration is deciding whose is best. There is plenty of time to come to a decision because it is one of those pastries that tastes even better as the days go by. Over the years Gerardo has refined his recipe to perfection, although he tells me his wife bakes a competing version every year. He did not, however, give me the family verdict.

When I asked Franco about wine accompaniments for these sumptuous dishes, he remembered his grandmother saying they drank only champagne and French wines with their meals. Well, why not? Should you, however, tire of the fizz, there are several worthy wines from Campania.

These elegant and sometimes extravagant recipes are obviously not intended as daily fare. Franco reserves them for the special dinners he gives at the request of his friends several times each year and for the gala receptions he hosts in the family *palazzo* on Piazza dei Martiri when there is an important cultural event in the city.

He does cook practically every night at home and if for some reason his wife has prepared dinner before he gets back from work, he feels deprived of his principal means of relaxation. Especially when his three children are home, Franco prepares a classical Neapolitan dish like *vermicelli in padella*, a thin spaghetti with a sauce of garlic, olive oil, capers, olives and anchovies crushed together in the pan and browned slowly so that their distinctive flavors combine. This is the kind of dish that is symbolic of the essence of Napoli where popular and aristocratic cuisines meet. And here, Franco affirms, "France had nothing to teach us."

149

MENU FIT FOR A KING

MOUSSE DI TONNO AI FAGIOLINI
Tuna mousse with green beans

POLPETTONE IN CROSTA
Meatloaf in a crust

INSALATA ALLA TORPINO
Walnut salad

PIZZE ANTONICCHIE
Miniature sweet pizzas

If you have the time and patience, you can line the entire outside of the mousse with long green beans. Place those that remain in the center and crumble some tuna over them. Peas would also be a good accompaniment to this dish.

The meatloaf is an elaborate recipe but delicious even without the crust. I remember my mother's cook made individual meatballs in the same way.

The little sweet pizzas have interesting contrasting flavors and are relatively simple to prepare.

Suggested Wines Try a fine white from the vineyards of Ravello along the Amalfi coast with the mousse; a rich, aged Taurasi with the meat course and with the sweet pizzas, an *amabile* Lacryma Christi from the slopes of Vesuvio.

MOUSSE DI TONNO AI FAGIOLINI
Tuna mousse with green beans

1 egg yolk
4 fl oz/1/2 cup/125 ml extra virgin olive oil
salt
2 fl oz/1/4 cup/50 ml whipping cream
1 lb/450 g tuna in oil
10 oz/300 g green beans, as long as possible

Put the egg yolk in a food processor. Add the oil in a thin stream and blend to form a thick mayonnaise. Add salt. Whip the cream to stiff peaks. Process the tuna through a food mill, add the mayonnaise and gently fold in the cream. Pour the mixture into a ring mold, smooth the surface and refrigerate for at least 6 hours.

Cook the beans in a pan of boiling salted water for about 10 minutes. Drain and refresh under cold running water. Unmold the mousse onto a platter. Decorate with the beans and serve.

POLPETTONE IN CROSTA
Meatloaf in a crust

For the pastry:
5 oz/10 tbsp/150 g butter
5 oz/1 cup/150 g plain (all-purpose) flour
For the filling:
1 lb/450 g lean minced (ground) beef
2 eggs
2 oz/1/2 cup/50 g grated Parmesan cheese
1 handful soft fresh breadcrumbs
1 glass dry sherry
salt and pepper
3 hard-boiled eggs
1 small onion
1 carrot
1/2 stalk celery
4 tbsp extra virgin olive oil
4 oz/125 g ham
4 tbsp milk
pinch of grated nutmeg

Prepare a puff pastry with the butter and flour (as explained on page 188). Refrigerate until ready to use.

Mix together the meat, 1 of the eggs, half the Parmesan, the breadcrumbs soaked in water and squeezed dry, half the sherry, salt and pepper. Roll out the mixture on a damp working surface into a rectangular shape 3/8 in/0.6 cm thick. Place the hard-boiled eggs in the middle and fold over the mixture to form a loaf.

Chop the vegetables and put in a flameproof casserole with the oil. Place the meatloaf on top and cook over moderate heat until the crust is golden. Add a couple of tablespoons of water, lower the heat, cover and cook for 1 hour, adding water from time to time, to keep the cooking juices moist. Remove the meatloaf and deglaze the casserole with the rest of the sherry. Strain the juices and keep warm.

Chop the ham and mix with the rest of the Parmesan, the second egg, milk and nutmeg. Spread the mixture over the meatloaf.

Roll out the puff pastry into a thin sheet. Put the meatloaf on top and wrap entirely with the pastry. Decorate with pastry scraps and bake in the oven at 375°F/190°C/Mark 5 for about 20 minutes until golden. Place on a platter and serve the pan juices separately.

INSALATA ALLA TORPINO
Walnut salad

1 head chicory (curly endive)
1 head red radicchio
3 1/2 oz/2 1/2 cups/100 g baby spinach leaves
1 fennel bulb
3 1/2 oz/100 g Parmesan cheese, finely sliced
1 bunch radishes
1 pomegranate
salt
1 tbsp red wine vinegar
4 tbsp extra virgin olive oil
4 oz/1 cup/125 g walnuts, chopped

Wash the chicory, radicchio and spinach and dry well. Clean and finely slice the fennel and radishes. Tear the salad leaves in pieces by hand and put in a serving bowl. Add the fennel, Parmesan, radishes and lastly the pomegranate seeds.

Dissolve the salt in the red wine vinegar, add olive oil and pour over the salad. Toss well, sprinkle with the chopped nuts and serve.

Mousse di tonno ai fagiolini

PIZZE ANTONICCHIE
Miniature sweet pizzas

5 oz/1 cup/150 g plain (all-purpose) flour
5 oz/²⁄₃ cup/150 g sugar
5 oz/150 g smoked provola (or Emmental) cheese, grated
1 egg plus 2 yolks
40 fl oz/5 cups/1 liter olive oil for frying
1 tbsp icing (confectioners') sugar

Place the flour on a working surface. Mix in the sugar and grated cheese and shape into a mound. Make a well in the center and pour in the eggs and yolks. Mix with a fork, and when the eggs are absorbed, knead the dough for about 10 minutes. (Or mix all the ingredients in a food processor.)

Roll out the dough into a sheet about ⅛ in/0.25 cm thick. Using a fluted pastry wheel, cut into circles about 3 in/8 cm in diameter.

In an iron frying pan heat the oil to just before smoking point (it is ready when a small piece of bread dropped in the oil forms little bubbles on the edges). Fry the pizzas, a few at a time, until they turn golden (they should float on top of the oil). Drain in a slotted spoon over paper towels. Arrange on a serving dish, sprinkle with the icing sugar and serve piping hot.

MENU FOR NAPOLI NOVANTANOVE

〜

PROVOLONE ALLA BARRACCO
Round of provolone cheese filled with rigatoni

UOVA ALLA VILLEROY
Deep-fried breaded eggs

FAGIOLINI IN SALSA DI PEPERONI
Green beans in a yellow pepper sauce

CHARLOTTE DI CASTAGNE
Chestnut dessert

If your cheese shop does not import provolone, use a sharp, aged cheese that has a form and crust suitable for hollowing out and filling which is really a delectable way to serve this pasta. (The pasta is also delicious served in a bowl.)

The trick with the famous breaded eggs, once you have them in their batter (in itself a feat), is to get their yolks to come out hot but still runny. I often take the easy way out and substitute chicken breasts. Any firm vegetable, such as artichokes, fennel, aubergine (eggplant), is also delicious fried in this batter.

In Italy we can afford to be lavish with chestnuts as they flourish from north to south.

Suggested Wines Stay with the remarkable Fiano di Avellino for the first three courses. It is dry and smooth and light straw-yellow in color. With dessert serve the sherry-like Amber Drops from the island of Ischia.

PROVOLONE ALLA BARRACCO
Round of provolone cheese filled with rigatoni

1 entire round of provolone cheese, about 2½ lb/2 kg
2 oz/50 g dried porcini mushrooms
5 oz/10 tbsp/150 g butter
8 oz/225 g beef stewing meat cut into bite-size pieces
8 oz/225 g veal stewing meat, cut into bite-size pieces
salt and 1 tbsp whole white peppercorns
1 bay leaf
1 carrot, peeled and minced
1 onion, chopped
2 stalks celery, minced
2 tbsp plain (all-purpose) flour
8 fl oz/1 cup/225 ml white wine
2 chicken livers
10 oz/300 g rigatoni (short pasta)
3½ oz/scant 1 cup/100 g grated Parmesan cheese
2 hard-boiled eggs, chopped
3½ oz/100 g sweet sausage, diced

Cut the top off the provolone and reserve. Hollow out the inside carefully. Dice 3½ oz/100 g of the cheese and set aside. Save the rest for another use. (Refrigerated, it will keep at least 1 month.) Soak the mushrooms in a cup of cold water for 30 minutes. Drain and chop.

Heat 2 oz/4 tbsp/50 g of the butter in a small frying pan. Brown the stewing meats with a pinch of salt, the peppercorns and bay leaf. Add the vegetables and sauté a few minutes. Sprinkle with the flour. Add the white wine and mushrooms, cover and cook over low heat for about 2 hours or until the meat is tender but not falling apart. Add water a little at a time whenever necessary. You will need about 8 fl oz/1 cup/225 ml water.

Cut the chicken livers into pieces and sauté them with 1 oz/2 tbsp/30 g of the butter over high heat for a few minutes. Season to taste and keep warm.

Bring to the boil a pan of salted water and cook the rigatoni until *al dente*. Drain, then toss with the remaining butter and the Parmesan cheese.

Mix the pasta with the meat, chicken livers, eggs, sausage and diced provolone. Sauté for a couple of minutes over moderate heat. Fill the provolone with the rigatoni, replace the top and serve.

UOVA ALLA VILLEROY
Deep-fried breaded eggs

2 oz/4 tbsp/50 g butter
5 oz/1 cup/150 g plain (all-purpose) flour
16 fl oz/2 cups/450 ml milk
salt and pepper
2 tbsp grated Parmesan cheese
pinch of grated nutmeg
7 eggs plus 2 yolks
1 tbsp red wine vinegar
4 oz/1 cup/125 g dry breadcrumbs
40 fl oz/5 cups/1 liter olive oil, for frying

Melt the butter in a small frying pan over moderate heat, add 2 oz/½ cup/50 g of the flour and mix until well blended. Add the milk, a little at a time, and cook for half a minute until the béchamel thickens. Remove from the heat, season with salt, pepper, Parmesan and nutmeg, then mix in the 2 egg yolks. Remove from the heat and set aside.

Into a large, shallow saucepan pour enough water to come 2 in/5 cm up the sides. Add salt

and the vinegar and bring to a simmer. One by one, crack 6 of the eggs onto a slotted spoon and immerse in the boiling water. As soon as the white has cooked (2 minutes), dip into cold water and then gently mold some of the lukewarm béchamel around each one, coating well.

When the sauce has solidified, roll each egg in the remaining flour, then in the remaining egg beaten with a pinch of salt, and lastly in the breadcrumbs. Heat the oil to just below smoking point and cook the eggs for 2 minutes. Drain on paper towels and serve immediately.

FAGIOLINI IN SALSA DI PEPERONI
Green beans in yellow pepper sauce

2 yellow bell peppers
1 head of garlic
4 tbsp extra virgin olive oil
2¼ lb/1 kg green beans
1 tbsp chopped parsley
salt

Cook the peppers with the unpeeled garlic for 20 minutes in the oven at 400°F/200°C/Mark 6. Peel the peppers and discard the seeds. Peel the garlic. Blend them in a food processor with half the oil. Add salt, pour the sauce in a saucepan and reserve.

Cook the beans in a saucepan of salted, boiling water for about 5 minutes or until crisp but barely tender. Drain and sauté over low heat in a frying pan with the remaining oil for about 5 minutes. Heat the pepper sauce. Arrange the beans on a platter, pour over the sauce, sprinkle with the chopped parsley and serve.

CHARLOTTE DI CASTAGNE
Chestnut dessert

2¼ lb/1 kg chestnuts
1 bay leaf
3½ oz/7 tbsp/100 g butter
2 oz/½ cup icing (confectioners') sugar
10 oz/1½ cups/300 g granulated sugar
2 oz/½ cup/50 g cocoa powder
16 fl oz/2 cups/450 ml whipping cream
1 tsp almond oil

Put the chestnuts in a large saucepan, cover with water, add the bay leaf, cover and simmer for about 30 minutes. Remove the shell and the inner skin from the chestnuts, then purée through a food mill or food processor. In a large bowl, blend the butter and half the icing sugar with a wooden spoon until creamy. Heat 4 oz/½ cup/100 g of the granulated sugar with 2 tbsp water for a couple of minutes. Combine the sugar syrup, chestnut purée, and cocoa with the butter mixture.

Whip the cream with the rest of the icing sugar until firm, then arrange in a mound on a serving dish. Pass half the chestnut purée mixture through the food mill again, using the largest holes, and arrange around the whipped cream like a crown. Form the rest of the purée into large balls the size of walnuts.

Put the remaining sugar in a saucepan, add 2 tbsp water and cook until caramelized. Dip the chestnut balls in the caramelized sugar and rest on a plate greased with the almond oil. As soon as they are cool, use to decorate the top and around the base of the charlotte. Refrigerate until ready to serve.

Provolone alla Barracco

Sartù di riso
Uova alla Villeroy

MENU FOR A MONZÙ

SARTÙ DI RISO
Neapolitan rice mold

GRANATINE AL MARSALA
Meat patties in Marsala

PASSATO DI PATATE
Potato purée

LA PASTIERA DI MONZÙ MODUGNO
Ricotta cake

The traditional *sartù* is tall and narrow in shape and a variety of ingredients can be combined with the rice. This recipe uses beef, veal, mushroom and tongue, but sweetbreads are also particularly good in a sartù. The dish takes time to compose but is not difficult or complicated. All the work can be done ahead of time and the mold baked at the last minute.

The elegant meat patties are another variation in the use of chopped meat in the recipes of the *cucina alto-borghese*. In the South, especially, imagination in the kitchen has had to make up for lack of meat in the larder. Historically, Italians have never been steak and potato eaters, but meatloaf, meatballs, meat rolls with a creamy purée, yes.

Because the Pastiera is the traditional Neapolitan Easter cake, every family has its own variation. I especially enjoyed this recipe from Monzù Modugno.

Suggested Wines Serve a superior dry Rosso from Ravello and with the cake, another bottle of sweet tears of Christ, Lacryma Christi, from Vesuvio.

SARTÙ DI RISO
Neapolitan rice mold

1 carrot
1 celery stalk
1 small onion
4 oz/8 tbsp/125 g butter
1 lb/500 g Arborio rice
35 fl oz/4⅓ cups/1 liter meat broth (page 189)
½ tsp powdered saffron
5 oz/1¼ cups/150 g grated Parmesan cheese
10 oz/300 g lean beef
4 tbsp extra virgin olive oil
4 tbsp plain (all-purpose) flour
1 small glass dry Marsala
10 oz/300 g minced (ground) veal
1 egg
3½ oz/100 g fresh button mushrooms
3½ oz/100 g cured tongue or ham
1 black truffle
3 oz/¾ cup/100 g shelled peas
2 oz/½ cup/50 g dry breadcrumbs
salt and pepper

Chop the carrot, celery and onion. Heat two-thirds of the butter in a saucepan and stir-fry half the vegetables. Add the rice and let it take on flavor for a couple of minutes over low heat. Cook for 15 minutes, adding enough broth to keep the rice just covered during cooking. Add the saffron dissolved in 1 tbsp water, turn off the heat, add half the remaining butter, three-quarters of the Parmesan, mix well and pour the rice onto a flat surface to cool.

Cut the beef into bite-size pieces and fry with the rest of the vegetables and half the oil. When it has taken on color, mix in half the flour, the Marsala, salt and pepper, cover and cook for about 2 hours over low heat, adding a little water from time to time in order to keep the cooking juices moist.

Mix the veal with the egg and the rest of the Parmesan, form into balls the size of walnuts, roll in the remaining flour and cook in a saucepan with the rest of the butter (reserving

1 oz/2 tbsp/25 g) until golden. Slice the mushrooms and cook in the remaining oil for 5 minutes over moderate heat.

Dice the tongue (or ham) and the truffle. Boil the peas for a couple of minutes in salted water and drain.

Grease a deep ovenproof dish with the remaining butter and coat with the breadcrumbs. Make a layer of rice about 1 in/3 cm high and top with successive layers of meat sauce, veal balls and all the other ingredients. Bake in the oven at 350°F/180°C/Mark 4 for about 1 hour. Turn out onto a platter and serve.

GRANATINE AL MARSALA
Meat patties in Marsala

1 handful soft fresh breadcrumbs
1 glass milk
1¾ lb/600 g lean minced (ground) beef
1 egg yolk
2 oz/½ cup/50 g grated Parmesan cheese
3½ oz/7 tbsp/100 g butter
3 tbsp chopped ham
2 tbsp chopped parsley
2 tbsp plain (all-purpose) flour
4 fl oz/½ cup/125 ml dry Marsala
salt and pepper

Soak the breadcrumbs in the milk and squeeze dry. Put in a bowl and add the meat, egg yolk, Parmesan, salt and pepper and mix well.

Soften three-quarters of the butter with a wooden spoon, then blend in the ham and parsley. Make 6 large meatballs with the beef mixture, and enclose within each one some of the ham mixture. Press down to flatten, then dust with flour on both sides.

Heat the remaining butter in a frying pan, and cook the meatballs for a couple of minutes on each side. Add the Marsala, reduce the heat and cook for about 5 minutes more, turning gently from time to time. Arrange on a platter with the potato purée and serve.

PASSATO DI PATATE
Potato purée

3 lb/1.5 kg potatoes
3½ oz/7 tbsp/100 g butter
8 fl oz/1 cup/225 ml milk
salt

Boil the potatoes in their skins and peel while still hot. Mash the potatoes using a mixer or food mill, add salt and butter, then beat with a whisk over low heat until the butter has melted. Add the milk, a little at a time, beating continuously, and continue to heat for a couple of minutes. Arrange around the meat patties and serve.

LA PASTIERA DI MONZÙ MODUGNO
Ricotta cake

For the filling:
7 oz/1 cup/200 g spelt (wheat grain)
6 fl oz/¾ cup/180 ml milk
grated peel of ½ orange
pinch of ground cinnamon
4 oz/½ cup/125 g granulated sugar
2 oz/¼ cup/50 g candied fruit, e.g. citron peel, cherries
10 oz/1¼ cups/300 g ricotta cheese
2 eggs
½ tsp orange blossom extract
1 tbsp icing (confectioners') sugar
For the short pastry dough:
7 oz/scant 1½ cups/200 g plain (all-purpose) flour
3½ oz/7 tbsp/100 g butter
2 egg yolks
4 oz/½ cup/100 g granulated sugar

Rinse the grain in cold water. Drain and cook over low heat for about 20 minutes with the milk, grated orange peel, cinnamon and 1 tbsp of the granulated sugar.

Finely dice the candied fruit, mix into the ricotta, add the remaining sugar, the eggs, the grain mixture and the orange extract diluted in 1 tbsp of water.

La pastiera di Monzù Modugno

Prepare the short pastry dough (as explained on page 188). Roll out three-quarters of it to line a 9 in/23 cm buttered and lightly floured spring-clip (springform) pan. Pour in the ricotta filling. Roll out the remaining dough, cut in strips and lay over the cake in a latticework design. Bake in the oven at a 350°F/180°C/Mark 4 for about 45 minutes until it turns golden. Allow to cool, sprinkle with icing sugar and serve.

PUGLIA

VILLA REALE A LECCE

*Simple pleasures of a baroque city at the home of
Count and Countess Pierandrea and Gloria Reale*

One of Italy's most charming features is that within a relatively small geographical area it contains a most amazing diversity and variety of cultures. This makes possible the pleasurable experience of being a tourist in your own native land. So, one hot day during the last week of August, while the rest of Italy was cooling off either at the sea or in the mountains, a friend and I, like mad dogs and Englishmen, took to the deserted *autostrada* and headed for the deep south of the peninsula.

Gloria Reale, a woman with whom I had become friends while our families were skiing in Cortina, had been insisting for years that I come visit her in Lecce, one of Italy's most celebrated cities. This "Florence of the South" is just a day's drive from where I live in Lombardia and Toscana but in a region of the country that is somewhat inaccessible and remote. Puglia forms the heel of the proverbial

*Field of red-flowered fodder under Puglia's ancient
olive trees and above, Villa Reale*

161

the "spur" of the Italian boot, near the breathtakingly beautiful Gargano promontory, through thousands of acres of wheat fields. Foggia, at its center, was already a granary in Greek and Roman times and today the area's many flour mills and factories produce Italy's best pasta. There are well-known commercial companies and smaller family-run businesses whose fine products never left the South until quite recently when they were discovered by Northern tourists like myself. Now certain brands are to be found in the gourmet food stores of the big cities. Not only is the quality excellent, it has a breadlike flavor and real body, but it is made in a variety of uncommon shapes. I shall load the trunk of my car with a supply to bring back home.

This commercial excellence has not undermined the established tradition of homemade pasta. The women of Puglia are renowned for their *orecchiette*, little ears, made by pressing the thumb on a tiny circle of dough. The hollow of the "ear" serves as a receptacle for the juices of the sauce. Pasta in Puglia is more often than not seasoned with sautéd vegetables, cauliflower, sweet peppers, broccoli, asparagus, artichokes and even potatoes. I have noticed that often when these dishes are announced the vegetable gets top billing as, for example,

The drawing room of Villa Reale

Traditional wooden dolls

Italian boot and Lecce lies practically at its very end, surrounded on three sides by the Adriatic and Ionian seas. This was a territory of *Magna Graecia*, Greek Italy, and is a different South from Napoli and the islands of Sicilia and Sardegna. In the Salento, as the southern tip of the region is called, there are still festivals in which *tarantati* dance the mysterious and erotic *tarantella*, originally thought to be both the cure for and the effect of tarantism, a sort of Saturday Night Fever brought on by the poison of the tarantula. Not far from Bari, the

immense and industrial seaport capital of Puglia, are the *trulli*, curious and picturesque, prehistoric stone habitations, many still lived in, with conical roofs whose tips are whitewashed and decorated with ancient mystical symbols. The people of Puglia tend to be tall and dignified in stature, a handsome race who manifest their Hellenistic ancestry as well as their present prosperity. They are more reserved than the Neapolitans yet evince Southern warmth and cordiality.

Coming from the North one enters Puglia at

turnip tops with orecchiette, rather than the other way round.

This primacy of the vegetable is characteristic of the region's cooking and it is easy to understand why as we drive across the fertile plain of Bari. Here olives, grapes, cereals, nuts, fruits and an astonishing variety of vegetables are produced in great abundance. Much of the fruit is canned or made into jam and dried fruit from Puglia is prized all over Italy for its moist, even juicy, texture. I especially like the apricots, and dried fruit marinated in the region's rare red dessert wine, Aleatico di Puglia, makes an unusual and easy dessert. The most famous of these products are *fichi mandorlati*, dried figs stuffed with almonds, seasoned with a few fennel seeds and baked in an oven. Ask for ones *ben cotti*, well cooked, which will have a rich, dark brown color.

A little further along is Brindisi where the Roman Appian Way ended and from whose harbor boats still sail for the overnight voyage to the Greek islands. This is melon territory and a sweet winter variety from these parts arrives as far north as my greengrocer's in Milano. They are harvested while still unripe and you sometimes see them hanging from the walls of houses in a cool, dry spot where they will keep until Christmas and even into the New Year. They have a sweet, firm flesh, ideal for an antipasto of *prosciutto e melone*.

In this area are many *masserie*, ancient, large farm houses and buildings where you can still buy the traditional regional cheeses. An unusual one is *burrata*, a pear-shaped sheep's cheese which encloses a lump of fresh, sweet butter. When you cut a slice you get butter and cheese all in one. A real peasant's cheese is dry ricotta, salted and aged and delicious crumbled over hot *pasta pugliese*. Also typical is *treccia*, lovely strands of braided mozzarella, and this region has a great number of smoked cheeses as well.

The hour's drive from Brindisi to Lecce is almost entirely through uninterrupted groves of olives. In a region that often appears to be an

The whitewashed town of Ostuni

endless vineyard, here the olive tree seems to outnumber the vine. (Puglia is Italy's largest producer of table grapes and Lecce of olive oil.) It is not the small, twisted tree one sees scattered throughout the hills of Toscana but one that grows to massive and majestic stature in this hot climate. They produce a fatter olive and a more abundant crop than the Tuscan variety and their excellent oil is smooth and mellow. Seasoned with anchovy and garlic it makes a perfect sauce for a *pinzimonio pugliese*, slices of crisp, raw vegetables, especially ones that are slightly bitter like chicory, endive, escarole and green radicchio, dipped in the olive oil before munching.

Arriving from the direction of Brindisi you enter the old walled city of Lecce through Porta Napoli, one of its three ancient portals. Its narrow streets and many small piazzas are lined with churches, palaces and public buildings decorated in an amazing and unique baroque style. The particular local stone is

extremely malleable and this quality gave great flexibility to the creative imagination and technical skill of the city's architects and artisans. The result is a richness of ornamentation on façades and interiors that continually delights with its golden twists and curves and intertwinings. It is joyful and unaffected, never pretentious or kitsch.

Modern Lecce is no sleepy, southern town with merely a curious artistic past. It has the bustling air of a prosperous provincial capital. Youth is much in evidence here. There are several university faculties, including banking, one of only two in all of Italy.

My friend, Gloria Reale, has invited us for Lecce's three-day celebration in honor of its patron saints, Oronzo, Giusto and Fortunato. Gloria is a Roman by birth who moved to Lecce when she married her husband, Pierandrea. They live just outside the city walls, in a superb nineteenth-century villa that is surrounded by over fifteen acres of park and

Trulli near Locorotondo

formal Italian gardens, one of the earliest masterpieces of the renowned Florentine landscape architect, Piero Porcinai. Here they have raised their five sons. Pierandrea owns and manages a large tobacco plantation, another of Lecce's principal crops, and is president of the Italian Tobacco Growers Association.

Lecce is a town to visit on foot and Gloria, who knows and appreciates her city as only an adopted resident can, is the perfect guide. Early every morning, while the air is still fresh, we set out on our walking tour, starting from Piazza Sant'Oronzo, which seems to be where Lecce gathers. First stop, a cappuccino and hot pastry at Café Alvino, a Lecce institution. Already it is full of Leccesi doing the same as we. The city seems to have a thriving café society as there are two other establishments on the piazza teeming with life. From the luscious selection of pastries Gloria recommends one that is shaped like a tiny loaf of bread with a soft golden crust and a delicious sweet ricotta filling.

Even on first acquaintance you notice that this city has a superior tradition of pastry cooking. The favorite midday snack seems to be little round puff pastries filled with a creamy cheese sauce and a slice of tomato, called *rustici*. In the windows of every bar and bakery are slices of pizza, usually with a vegetable topping. I treated myself several times during my stay to one with thin slices of potato. Then, of course, there is the famous *pane pugliese*, immense rustic wheels with a hard golden crust and a chewy, porous interior. It is the quintessential picnic bread, especially the loaves made with olives kneaded into the dough. It was in Puglia at the end of the nineteenth century that an imaginative baker from Bari named Felice Lippoli invented the ice-cream sandwich or *gelato al forno*, two pieces of bread with a slice of ice cream in the center, sprinkled with sugar and candied fruits and baked in the oven.

During one of our strolls through Lecce Gloria brought us to a lovely convent of cloistered Benedictine nuns where a sublime surprise was in store for us. In the entrance hall there was a wooden turnstile in the wall, an ancient monastic device that allows the nuns to have commerce with the outside world without contact and remaining unseen. Gloria rang the bell and after considerable suspense, we heard footsteps and the rustling of a nun's habit on the other side. A lilting voice saluted us with, "*Sia lodato Gesù Cristo!*" (May Jesus Christ be praised!) After a few words of greeting, Gloria asked the sister if we might buy "*un pesce di natale*," a Christmas fish, which seemed a strange request at the end of August. After another brief wait (it is not time but eternity that matters here), sister returned and revolved the turnstile in our direction. On it was a most marvelous confection made of sugar and almonds in the shape of a fish with scales even, and a coffee bean for an eye and, as we later discovered, pear jam hidden in the center. The fish was an arcane symbol of the early Christians for Christ (based on a Greek anagram) and at Easter the sisters make the same confection in the form of the Paschal lamb.

Almonds are a major crop of Puglia and are eaten in a variety of ways, particularly as a sweet. Much in evidence on the stalls that filled the main streets and piazzas for the feast-days were bags of almonds roasted in their shells as well as a kind of sugar and almond torrone bar that resembles a stick of crystal candy. And for a late afternoon reviver when we felt our feet and spirits lagging, Gloria introduced us to a refreshing local drink, *latte di mandorle*, almond milk, homemade from pounded nuts.

In the cafés of Lecce they serve another stimulating summer drink, *caffè con ghiaccio*, coffee with ice, which is *not* the same as iced coffee, *caffè freddo*, a sugary drink made well ahead in large quantities and kept in the refrigerator. Instead, *caffè con ghiaccio* is brought to the table in two containers, a glass with ice cubes and a cup of hot, fresh espresso that you must pour over the ice without delay and drink immediately. There is a second when the coffee is thoroughly chilled but has not lost any of its freshly-brewed aroma or flavor and that is the moment you try to capture. In the South, pleasure as well as coffee is still an art.

One morning we made the short drive to Gallipoli, a picturesque medieval city of sun-baked, whitewashed houses completely covering a tiny island in the Ionian sea just a stone's throw from the mainland. It is a fishing town and is famous for its soup, *zuppa di pesce alla gallipolina*. We tried it in a restaurant right off the lively fish market. It is made from a recipe

Rustic sconelike bread found in Lecce

whose ancestry goes back to the Greeks and contains an indescribable variety of fish cooked in olive oil, onion, vinegar and seasoned with pepper. Gloria brought back a fresh *dentice*, one of the Mediterranean's finest fish. For dinner that evening she baked it simply in olive oil and white wine, seasoned with rosemary and parsley.

On two evenings we attended theatrical performances that were part of the special program of cultural events organized for the three-day festival. Lecce has an ancient tradition of theater certainly going back to the Greeks. Just off Piazza Sant'Oronzo there is a Roman amphitheater and practically hidden in the back streets of the city is a smaller Roman theater. One evening we were privileged to watch the performance of a play in the local dialect from the garden terrace of one of Gloria's friends that overlooks the theater. On the menu for the supper afterward, accompanying the main course of small slices of stuffed goose neck, was another vegetable specialty of Puglia, beetroot (beet). Here it grows wild as well as in the garden and both its leaves and its roots are eaten. The leaves are cooked much like spinach, except they take longer. Our hostess baked the beetroot in foil, which preserves its sweetness, dressed it with a savory vinaigrette and sprinkled the wine-red slices with fresh mint.

With our after-dinner coffee we were treated to another Lecce delicacy called *cotognata leccese*, a sweet quince preserve deep rose red in color and so dense in texture it can be sliced into squares and served like candy. It is made by reducing the puréed fruit in sugar, spreading the paste about half an inch thick on trays and letting it dry in the sun. In the stores of Lecce it comes packed in little woven wooden boxes – yet another gastronomic souvenir to take back home with me.

For the final evening of the festival Pierandrea and Gloria gave a dinner party. The tables were arranged on the terrace of their magnificent garden and set with lovely old Grottaglie

Regional cheeses including pecorino, cacio ricotta, pampanella and ricotta forte, produced at the Masseria Carestia, friends of the Reale family

porcelain, a treasured ceramic of the region. For the first course Gloria served two native vegetables, curly endive and broad (fava) beans prepared in a delicious and elegant mold. The main course was one of the very few regional meat dishes, tiny chops of exquisite milk-fed lamb baked in a sauce of tomato, mushroom, anchovy and capers. While we enjoyed our dessert we watched the spectacular fireworks display (another specialty of the South) that brought to a brilliant conclusion the feast-day celebrations and our visit to Lecce.

MENU FOR SAN FORTUNATO

PUNTARELLE E FINOCCHI ALL'AGRO
Chicory and fennel in anchovy lemon sauce

DENTICE AL VINO BIANCO
White fish baked in wine

FONDI DI CARCIOFO DORATI
Baked stuffed artichokes

GELATO DI MIELE E NOCI
Honey and nut ice cream

Curly endive and escarole (or green radicchio if you can find it) are good substitutes or additions to this raw vegetable platter. *Dentice* is a Mediterranean fish but another fresh, white firm-fleshed fish of an appropriate size can be used as an alternative.

Before I acquired an ice-cream machine I used to make gelato by freezing the mixture, then putting it through a processor and immediately back into the freezer.

Suggested Wines Locorotondo is a good local wine for fish.

PUNTARELLE E FINOCCHI ALL'AGRO
Chicory and fennel in anchovy lemon sauce

18 oz/500 g chicory (curly endive) or green radicchio
3 fennel bulbs
2 anchovy fillets in oil
juice of 1 lemon
2 garlic cloves, finely chopped
6 tbsp extra virgin olive oil
salt and pepper

Separate out the individual leaves of the greens and place in a bowl of iced water.

Cut off the tops of the fennel, and discard the discolored outside stalks. Cut each bulb almost into quarters, but leave them attached at the base. Drain the greens and place on a serving dish.

In a bowl, mash the anchovy fillets, add a pinch of salt and pepper and the lemon juice. Mix to dissolve the salt, add the oil and blend well. Invite your guests to dip the two vegetables into the sauce.

DENTICE AL VINO BIANCO
White fish baked in wine

1 white firm-fleshed fish, about 4½ lb/2 kg
1 sprig rosemary
1 tbsp red wine vinegar
4 tbsp extra virgin olive oil
1 lemon, sliced
1 glass white wine
1 tbsp chopped parsley
salt and pepper

Clean the fish. Dip the rosemary in the vinegar, sprinkle with salt and pepper and place inside the fish.

Place the fish in an ovenproof dish with half the oil and cover with the lemon slices. Add salt and pepper, pour over the rest of the olive oil and the white wine and cook in the oven at 400°F/200°C/Mark 6 for about 20 minutes, basting frequently with the cooking juices. Sprinkle with the parsley and serve.

FONDI DI CARCIOFO DORATI
Baked stuffed artichokes

6 globe artichokes
juice of 1 lemon
2 onions

Dentice al vino bianco
Puntarelle e finocchi all'agro

4 tbsp extra virgin olive oil

pinch of grated nutmeg

2 egg yolks

6 tbsp grated Parmesan cheese

2 tbsp dry breadcrumbs

salt and pepper

Prepare the artichokes, peeling away all but the tender edible leaves and cutting out the inedible centers to expose the hearts so that the artichokes can be stuffed.

Place each one immediately in a bowl of cold water with lemon juice to avoid discoloration. Blanch the prepared artichokes for 5 minutes in lightly salted water. Drain and pat dry.

Slice the onions and stir-fry over low heat in a saucepan with half the oil. Add salt, pepper and nutmeg, mix and remove from heat. Pass through a food mill, add the egg yolks and the Parmesan and mix well.

Oil an ovenproof dish and pour in half a glass of water. Fill the artichokes with the purée, sprinkle with the breadcrumbs, season with the rest of the oil and cook in the oven at 400°F/200°C/Mark 6 for 20 minutes before serving.

GELATO DI MIELE E NOCI
Honey and nut ice cream

6 egg yolks

7 oz/1 cup less 2 tbsp/200 g sugar

6 tbsp honey

10 fl oz/1¼ cups/300 ml milk

3 oz/¾ cup/100 g walnuts, shelled and chopped

Beat the egg yolks with the sugar in a double boiler, stirring constantly until the mixture thickens. Add the honey and milk, still stirring, and cook until the new mixture thickens. Allow to cool before transferring to an ice cream machine. When the ice cream is made, put it on a platter, sprinkle with the chopped nuts and serve.

MENU FOR SAN GIUSTO

PENNE CON I CARCIOFI
Short pasta with artichokes

COLLO D'OCA RIPIENO
Stuffed goose neck

BARBABIETOLE ALLA MENTA
Beetroot (beets) with mint

FRUTTA SECCA AL VINO BIANCO
Dried fruit marinated in sweet white wine

Small spring artichokes are best in this pasta dish. It is, however, a good opportunity to use more mature ones, whose leaves simply have to be peeled a little further. I am fond of mixing sautéd firm-textured vegetables with short pasta: fennel, broccoli and cauliflower also work well.

Chicken necks can be stuffed in the same way as the goose neck, and both are delicious served cooled with mayonnaise.

Normally Italians do not mix mustard with olive oil and vinegar to season salads or vegetables – we want to taste the flavor of the oil. With beetroot (beets), however, because they are sweet, a pinch of mustard is nice.

In Puglia the dried fruit would be marinated in Aleatico, but any fine dessert wine can be used.

Suggested Wines An unusual and fine choice would be the unique rosé, Five Roses, made by Leone De Castris. It is a dry, fragrant wine given its name, Burton Anderson recounts in the Mitchell Beazley *Pocket Guide to Italian Wines*, by American officers during the war who liked it so much they awarded it one rose more than a popular bourbon.

PENNE CON I CARCIOFI
Short pasta with artichokes

6 small, tender globe artichokes

5 fl oz/⅔ cup/150 ml extra virgin olive oil

3½ oz/100 g pancetta

2 cloves garlic, chopped

1 lb/450 g penne (short pasta)

6 tbsp grated Parmesan cheese

salt and pepper

Clean the artichokes, slice lengthwise into halves, quarters or even smaller, depending on size and cook in a saucepan with half the oil over low heat for 15 minutes or until tender, stirring occasionally.

Brown the pancetta in a large, deep frying pan over moderate heat with the remaining olive oil and the garlic. Cook the pasta until *al dente* in a pan of salted, boiling water. Drain and add to the pancetta. Add the artichokes, cover, and cook for a couple of minutes over moderate heat, stirring once or twice. Pour into a bowl, sprinkle with Parmesan and serve.

COLLO D'OCA RIPIENO
Stuffed goose neck

1 goose neck (or chicken neck)

3½ oz/100 g ham

3½ oz/100 g mortadella

1 large handful soft fresh breadcrumbs

1 glass plus 1 tbsp milk

1 hard-boiled egg, chopped, and 1 whole egg

2 oz/½ cup/50 g grated Parmesan cheese

12 oz/350 g lean minced (ground) pork

½ lb/225 g lean minced (ground) veal

1 tbsp chopped fresh thyme

1 carrot

1 onion

1 celery stalk

2 cloves

1 bunch parsley

1 bay leaf

1 egg yolk

3½ fl oz/scant ½ cup/100 ml extra virgin olive oil
juice of 1 lemon
salt and pepper

Bone out the neck of the goose. Chop the ham and mortadella. Soak the breadcrumbs in the milk (reserving the tbsp) and squeeze dry. Mix the meats and breadcrumbs with the chopped egg, the whole egg, the Parmesan, and salt and pepper. Stuff the neck of the goose with this mixture and wrap in muslin (cheesecloth).

Bring to the boil a pan of salted water, add the carrot, onion, celery, cloves, parsley, thyme and bay. Cook for 30 minutes, add the goose neck and continue cooking for about 40 minutes.

In a processor, beat the egg yolk, add the oil in a stream and blend until a mayonnaise is formed. Add salt and pepper and dilute with the lemon juice and the tablespoon of milk.

Remove the goose neck from the pan, unwrap and leave to cool. Cut into slices, arrange on a platter, pour over the mayonnaise and serve.

BARBABIETOLE ALLA MENTA
Beetroot (beets) with mint

3 large beetroot (beets)
1 tbsp red wine vinegar
1 tsp powdered mustard
4 tbsp extra virgin olive oil
handful of mint leaves
salt

Wash the beetroot and wrap each in foil. Cook in the oven at 350°F/180°C/Mark 4 for about 1 hour until tender. Unwrap, peel and leave to cool. Slice and arrange on a platter.

Dissolve the salt in the vinegar, add the mustard, mix well and add the olive oil. Pour the dressing over the beets, sprinkle with the mint and serve.

Barbabietole alla menta

FRUTTA SECCA AL VINO BIANCO
Dried fruit marinated in sweet white wine

10 oz/300 g mixed dried fruit, apricots, prunes, figs
4 oz/½ cup/125 g sugar
½ bottle sweet white wine

Boil the dried fruit with the sugar in water to cover over low heat for about 10 minutes and drain. When cool, put the fruit in a deep bowl and pour over enough wine to cover completely. Marinate for 24 hours. Serve in goblets with some of the wine.

MENU FOR SANT'ORONZO

SFORMATO DI FAVE E CICORIA
Curly endive and broad (fava) bean mold

COSTOLETTE D'AGNELLO AI CAPPERI
Lamb chops in caper sauce

FORMELLE DI SPINACI
Little spinach molds

PERE CARAMELLATE
Caramelized pears

The recipe for the first course takes two native and humble Apulian ingredients, curly endive and broad (fava) beans, and presents them in a form that is still simple but also elegant.

In Italy we eat very young lamb. If yours is more mature, it will give off liquid while being baked. In that case, toward the end of cooking open the parchment (silicon) paper so that it can evaporate.

Peaches are also delicious and pleasing when caramelized in the same way as the pears in this recipe.

Suggested Wines With the lamb serve an aged Torre Quarto, one of Puglia's most distinguished reds. Leone De Castris also makes a port-like red dessert wine called Negrino that your guests might enjoy sipping after dessert.

SFORMATO DI FAVE E CICORIA
Curly endive and broad (fava) bean mold

3½ oz/100 g pancetta
1 onion
4 tbsp extra virgin olive oil
1¼ lb/600 g broad (fava) beans, podded (husked)
½ glass white wine
1 small round (Boston) lettuce, shredded
2 large potatoes

2 eggs
1¼ lb/600 g curly endive
3½ oz/100 g prosciutto, finely sliced
salt

Chop the pancetta and onion, stir-fry in half the olive oil until transparent. Add the beans, reserving a few for garnish, white wine, pinch of salt, cover and cook over low heat until the beans are tender. Add the shredded lettuce and continue cooking for 5 minutes. Purée the mixture through a food mill or food processor.

Boil the potatoes, drain, peel and purée while still hot. Mix together the two purées, add the eggs and pour into an oiled mold. Place the mold in a pan of water and bake at 350°F/180°C/Mark 4 for about 45 minutes.

About 20 minutes before serving, blanch the curly endive, drain and put in a saucepan with the prosciutto and the remaining oil. Cook over low heat for about 10 minutes, stirring occasionally. Add salt. Unmold the purée of beans on to a platter, arrange the curly endive around and serve.

COSTOLETTE D'AGNELLO AI CAPPERI
Lamb chops in caper sauce

1 tbsp dried porcini mushrooms
6 ripe plum tomatoes
1 tbsp capers
3 anchovy fillets in oil
6 lamb chops, thickly cut
3 tbsp extra virgin olive oil
salt and pepper

Soak the mushrooms in water for about 30 minutes. Drain, squeeze dry and chop. Drop the tomatoes into boiling water for a few seconds, drain, peel and chop. Chop the capers and mash the anchovy fillets.

Lightly oil 6 pieces of parchment (silicon) paper and place a chop on each, followed by some tomato, mushroom, anchovy and capers. Add salt and pepper and pour over the rest of the oil. Wrap up each parcel and cook in the

oven at 450°F/230°C/Mark 8 for 15 minutes. Open each parcel, arrange the chops on a platter and serve.

FORMELLE DI SPINACI
Little spinach molds

3 lb/1.5 kg fresh spinach
4 tbsp extra virgin olive oil
3 eggs
2 oz/½ cup/50 g grated Parmesan cheese
pinch of grated nutmeg
salt and pepper

Clean the spinach, keeping the stems on. Blanch for a couple of minutes in a pan of salted, boiling water. Drain and squeeze dry.

Heat 3 tbsp of the olive oil in a casserole and cook the spinach for about 5 minutes, stirring frequently. Chop finely. Transfer to a bowl, add the eggs, Parmesan, nutmeg, salt and pepper and mix together well.

Fill 6 individual oiled molds with the spinach mixture, and smooth the surface. Cook in a pan of water in the oven at 350°F/180°C/Mark 4 for 20 minutes, until a toothpick inserted in the center comes out dry. Unmold on to a plate and serve.

PERE CARAMELLATE
Caramelized pears

6 ripe pears
1 oz/2 tbsp/25 g butter
6 amaretti biscuits (cookies), crumbled
¼ cup raspberry jam (or jelly)
¼ cup granulated sugar

Peel the pears, halve lengthwise and remove the cores. Arrange cut side up in a buttered ovenproof dish. Mix the crumbled amaretti with the jam and fill the pears with the mixture. Sprinkle with sugar and bake in the oven at 400°F/200°C/Mark 6 for 15 minutes. Place under the grill (broiler) for a few minutes to caramelize the surface, then serve.

Sformato di fave e cicoria

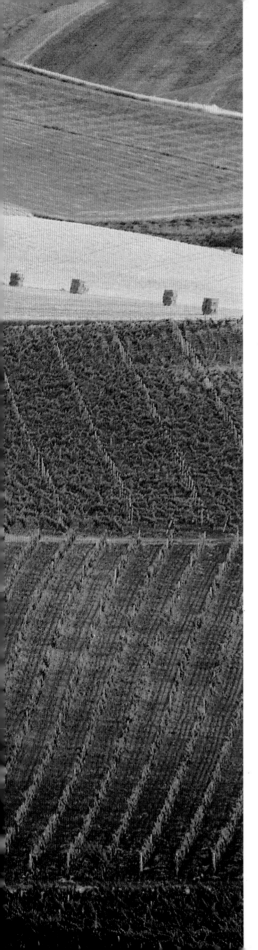

SICILIA

REGALEALI IN CALTANISSETTA

*Regaling with noble wines and a noble family in the country
estate and winery of Count Giuseppe Tasca d'Almerita*

For more reasons than one, Sicilia is the most fitting place to conclude our tour. The "one" is that it is literally the end of the line. Just a few miles off its southern shore lies Africa. On a clear day you can see its coastline and on any day its influence can be felt, in art, architecture, physiognomy and even gastronomy.

The other more compelling reason is that this, the largest Mediterranean island, is a place where all the qualities (and defects!) of Italy seem to be present in their most intense and colorful form. Luigi Barzini wrote that "Sicilia is the schoolroom model of Italy for beginners," but even the most advanced students of Italian civilization find it complex and intriguing.

Arriving in Sicilia is like entering a cornuco-

*The Tasca vineyards in central Sicilia,
and above, the villa at Regaleali*

pia. It virtually overflows with flowers, fruits and produce of every kind. It seems that all growing things (including *bambini*, who are the most beautiful here) thrive in this semitropical climate. My favorite time to visit is early spring – the end of March or the first days of April – when the part of Northern Italy where I live is still trying (usually without much success) to shake off the residue of winter. Here, instead, all is abloom: azaleas, mimosa, oleanders, acacia, hibiscus, cascading bougainvillaea, avenues of jacaranda, groves of almonds and pistachios, terraces of orange trees, tangerines and lemons, enormous gnarled olive trees with silvered leaves, vineyards thriving in the most unlikely plots and the ubiquitous prickly pear cactus in brilliant bloom. The Phoenicians aptly called the capital of this cornucopia "Ziz," meaning "Flower." It is no wonder that Palermo boasts the oldest and still one of the finest botanical gardens in Europe, acres of avenues with every imaginable and unimagin-

able exotic tree and plant.

Palermo's food market overflows onto a dozen streets in the old city center. This is only one of the many places on the island where East meets West and there are moments while walking through these narrow lanes crammed with food stalls when I feel I might be in Tunis or Marrakesh. By contrast the equally fabulous but relatively structured food market of Firenze seems positively Teutonic. Here everything is in heaps and piles: lustrous vegetables of rich texture and color – white fennel, purple artichokes with extravagant foliage, scarlet radishes, mountains of gleaming red, yellow and green peppers; and the fruit – pyramids of blood oranges, some with their luscious flesh exposed, baskets of figs and great clusters of dates.

The amazing thing is that everything seems to be in flower and in season at the same time. Here the weather turns warm early. In Agrigento on the southern coast, the almond

Ragusa Ibla, a baroque hilltown in the southwest of Sicilia

blossom festival welcoming spring is held on the first Sunday of February and the arrival of fruits and vegetables from Sicilia at my greengrocer's in Milano during what seems like the dead of winter is the first harbinger of spring.

In the Sicilian kitchen this practically year-round exuberance of raw material is transformed into an equally effusive cuisine. A good place to start when speaking of the island's gastronomy is at the end of the meal, with dessert. The root of the Sicilian sweet tooth can probably be traced back to the Saracen invasion of the island in the ninth century. At any rate the taste for sophisticated sweets is deeply embedded in their culture and often assumes an even symbolic importance. Take, for example, just one of the internationally famous Sicilian desserts, *cannoli*. These are crunchy pastry "pipes" filled with creamy ricotta, candied fruit, pistachio nuts and chocolate. In all probability this sweet had its origins as an edible fertility symbol and, needless to say, it predates by a long while New York's Erotic Bakery. It is still traditional to eat them during the period of *carnevale*, that celebration of winter turning to spring, death to new life. A Sicilian friend of mine recalls her grandmother's custom of making an extra batch of *cannoli* at Easter as gifts for the neighbors and always the sacred number of twelve, no more no less.

In any case, when in Sicilia remember to leave room for dessert and maybe even for an ice cream during the after-dinner promenade. It is reputed to be the best in the world and their sherbets certainly are. Order a double scoop of *gelsomino* (jasmin) if you want a taste of paradise.

If pastry is king of Sicilian gastronomy, then pasta, which allegedly had its origins here, is queen and the nourishing factor at the table. As any Sicilian will tell you, it is their wheat and flour that make the difference. In fact, Sicilian pasta has such a substantial flavor on its own that it requires little in the way of added enormous swordfish. They could not have been long out of the sea and I am sure it took more men to maneuver them to the stall than to land them in the first place. On my way back I noticed that their swords, like the arms of the vanquished, had proudly been put on display.

The best place I know for tasting the specialties of the Sicilian table is Regaleali, the country estate and winery of Count Giuseppe Tasca d'Almerita. In Sicilia *masserie* have a long-established tradition of combining fine food with fine wine. Regaleali excels in this, not only because Count Giuseppe makes excellent wine but also because he has employed for over thirty-five years one of Sicily's finest cooks, Mario Lo Menzo. The last time I was in Sicilia was for the wedding of one of Count Giuseppe's grandchildren, Donna Fabrizia Lanza di Mazzarino. The bride is probably the only person who may not be able to recall in delicious detail what Mario prepared for that extraordinary feast, served to three hundred guests at the family's splendid villa in Palermo.

Trompe-l'oeil wallpaper and marble statue in the Villa Tasca, Palermo

Portrait of Margherita di Savoia (1874)

ingredients. Sauces with meat and cheese are few. Instead, Sicilians favor aromatic seasonings, using their wealth of herbs and vegetables. *Pasta alle sarde*, the preferred pasta of Palermo, is a notable exception. It is made with sardines, fresh fennel, anchovies, saffron, raisins and pine nuts. The result is more harmonious than it perhaps sounds. It can also be layered and baked as a pie and is delicious served either hot or cold.

With so much enthusiasm put into what comes before and after, the second course seems to be of almost secondary importance. In general, Sicilians use relatively little meat in their diet. Various spicy sausages are common in the *cucina povera* and more sophisticated meat rolls and other elaborated dishes appear on the menus of the *cucina alto-borghese*. Of course, the island has a plentiful supply of fine fish and Sicilian tuna and swordfish are superior. The last time I was walking through the Palermo food market there was great excitement on the fishmongers' street at the arrival of a hand-drawn cart carrying three a great many as he is the recognized and sole heir to one of the legendary chefs of Sicilia, Giovanni Messina, who died at the age of eighty and had been with the Tasca family for forty years. During that time he cooked for literally thousands of illustrious guests, including the King of Italy, Umberto di Savoia, as well as Alfonso XII of Spain. Mario was his apprentice, then assistant, and before he died Messina publicly declared him "the only one to whom I have confided my secrets."

Mario is a hearty and handsome man in his early fifties and enjoys both the physical and professional stature of a great chef. As befits his role of recipient of a legendary tradition, he is a man who has a million culinary feats to recount. He still recalls the twelve days of preparation preceding the wedding banquet of Count Giuseppe's daughter, Costanza, to Prince Paolo di Camporeale. One of the dishes was a pâté that cost a patrimony. In order to obtain two to three kilograms it was necessary to begin with twenty-two kilograms of goose liver. This Messina ordered Mario to pound with a very heavy pestle in a large marble mortar until it had become a velvety pulp,

A porcelain Madonna encased in the wall for good luck

The farmhouse at Regaleali

Even a major national newspaper reported the menu in the next day's edition. There were bowls of rice pilaf, some with lobster and shrimp, others with fricasseed lamb; pasta in the form of vol-au-vents with black truffles and prosciutto; a swordfish mousse that even the bride would remember; baked hams; mutton roasts; platters of fish and a mille-feuille wedding cake.

This time I am going to Regaleali in order to participate in the ceremony at which Count Giuseppe will receive the French award of merit, "*Personnalité de l'année.*" Knowing Mario Lo Menzo, it will also be the gala occasion for the banquet of the year.

Marchesa Anna Lanza di Mazzarino, Count Giuseppe's daughter, has suggested that I drive from Palermo to Regaleali a day early with Mario who has come down to do some last-minute grocery shopping. It is well over an hour's drive and I am delighted to have this chance to discuss menus and recipes and cooking with Mario all to myself. Maybe he will even share a secret or two with me. He has almost fluid in consistency. It took him hours. Messina was pleased with the results of his apprentice's toil but commented that it would have tasted even more exquisite had it been made in the authentic eighteenth-century Sicilian way, with chicken liver instead of goose.

While listening to Mario reminiscing and discussing the menu and recipes for tomorrow's banquet, I realize that he represents a tradition of Sicilian cooking that is sometimes called the "baronial cuisine." It evolved over centuries of foreign domination, came into its own in the eighteenth century and continues even now in the kitchens of the island's great noble families. As in their bloodlines, so at their tables they amalgamated diverse foreign influences – Greek, Arab, French and Spanish – and created a uniquely Sicilian gastronomy.

Enjoyable company and interesting con- versation make the time pass quickly and before I know it we have passed through the entrance gates of Regaleali and are driving up the wide road that winds for several kilometers along gently rolling hills to Le Case Grandi, a picturesque grouping of ancient houses built around a large courtyard where the family lives. The name Regaleali derives from the Arabic "*Rahl Ali*," meaning the houses of Ali, and in origin it was probably a small Arab

Landscape of rolling arable land near Regaleali

village. From Le Case Grandi one enjoys a view for miles in all directions. We are practically at the geographical center of the island, the heartland of Sicilia, and there are gleaming fields of grain as far as the eye can see.

The some 1,200 acres of the Regaleali estate crown these hills and its precious jewel is 500 prime acres of vineyards that produce the estate's premium wines, exported all over the world. Behind Le Case Grandi are extensive winery buildings that house the ultimate in contemporary winemaking technology along-side ancient chestnut vats for ageing. The estate had been an ex-fiefdom twice its present size when it was acquired by the Tasca family in 1830. Their development of the land played an important role in nineteenth-century Sicilian agrarian reform and today it is considered an agronomical showpiece of the island.

We are greeted by Lucio Tasca, Count Giuseppe's son, who manages the estate with his father. Lucio is accompanied by his son, Giuseppe, Jr., who is studying viticulture and enology at a Northern Italian university and, it is hoped, will become the seventh generation of this Sicilian winemaking dynasty to direct Regaleali.

At the award ceremony on the following day, Count Giuseppe and his wife, Franca, are surrounded by the full complement of their family – four children, eleven grandchildren and two great-grandchildren. In the twenty years it has been given, only a dozen people in the sector of enology have been honored with this international distinction. This same year another winemaker of Italian origin has also been selected by the jury, California's Robert Mondavi.

A gala dinner for some eighty guests follows in the grand reception rooms of the winery. Mario has lived up to his reputation and it would definitely get my vote for "banquet of the year." There are four courses and several choices with each. I could have made a meal of the antipasti alone, and I almost did. Instead, I decided on the *degustazione* approach to take

me through to the finish without missing a dish. The first antipasti I tasted were yellow squash fritters seasoned with garlic, mint and a suggestion of cinnamon. The recipe reveals an Arabic influence and Mario had explained to me that usually these fritters are made with sugar and served as a feast-day dessert. Substituting garlic transforms them into a tasty way to begin a festive meal. The fresh mussels we had brought back with us from Palermo were next. These are the celebrated *cozze nere* cultivated in the waters off the southernmost tip of the island, where they are eaten raw like oysters with a squeeze of lemon. Mario had baked them briefly in breadcrumbs, Parmesan cheese, egg, parsley, lemon and olive oil. The third choice featured the famous Southern Italian cheese, caciocavallo, a specialty of Palermo, in the form of croquettes fried in "angel-hair" pasta. These delicious antipasti were washed down with an equally delicious white wine, Regaleali Nozze d'Oro, a com-memoration vintage produced on the occasion of the golden wedding anniversary of Count Giuseppe and Countess Franca. Their distin-guished profiles are on the elegant label printed in gold. Giuseppe Jr. tells me it is a blend of white grapes including a special clone of Sauvignon developed on the estate that will soon be registered as "Sauvignon Tasca."

Colorful Sicilian fruits and vegetables

While eating the pasta course I could almost imagine myself at a restaurant specializing in Californian cooking. The use of ingredients for the sauces seems so inventive, yet the recipes are centuries-old Sicilian classics – spaghetti with lentils, macaroni with cauliflower and black olives and *anelletti*, little hand-made pasta rings baked with aubergines (eggplant) and slices of hard-boiled egg. A young and fragrant Regaleali Rosato accompanied this course. It is made from the same grapes as their red wine and is a delicious and very superior rosé.

The main courses were masterly in both preparation and presentation. We began simp-ly, with a dish of fresh sardines baked in orange rind arranged on the platter in such a way that their shimmering silver highlighted slices of citrus. This was followed by *pasticcio di fagiano*, a marbled loaf of pheasant pâté served with a splendid stuffed specimen of the species to the side. The glazed medallions of chicken com-memorated the French contribution to Sicilian cuisine. They were presented in baskets woven out of dry spaghetti and decorated with frozen carnations and roses. The Bourbons would have been as pleased as we were. To do honor to these masterpieces Lucio selected an old vintage of Rosso del Conte, an elegant special reserve that experts consider Sicilia's grandest red.

I tried to remember that dessert was yet to come, but it was difficult when the mushrooms sautéd in Marsala wine arrived. Mario told me that to achieve the exquisite flavor of this uncomplicated dish the wine had to be "Marsala di Marsala." The type he used was the prestigious "*vergine*" because it is dry and smooth and has a rich wood aroma. "But, for cooking?" you may well ask. Well, this is Regaleali and Mario is in the kitchen. Two typical Sicilian salads followed, one made with fennel and the other with lemons dressed with olive oil and garnished with black peppers and parsley, both ideal for cleansing the palate for the event to come.

And it was divine: oranges cut into the shape of little baskets and filled with tangy

Chef Mario and his buffet spread

tangerine gelatine; a gâteau of watermelon ice cream covered with pistachio and almond glaze and decorated with candied fruit, and a grand finale of *cannoli*. We toasted the "Personality of the Year" with an excellent "experimental" spumante that Lucio tells me will be officially released in 1990. In the Renaissance spirit of his winemaking family, Count Giuseppe announced that he is developing a new fortified wine that he will present on the occasion of his

and Countess Franca's diamond wedding anniversary in 1994!

Early the next day Anna and I walk to where the shepherds are making cheese from the morning's milking. She wants to take away some fresh ricotta for breakfast and I would like to bring home some *pepato*, a Sicilian pecorino with whole black peppercorns. Along the way she tells me that she and her two sisters, Costanza and Rosemarie, are planning

to inaugurate a series of live-in cooking classes at Regaleali for English speakers. Mario would explain the day's menu and recipes, the sisters would supervise the execution and everyone would taste the results at lunch. This marvelous news, coming at the end of our tour and from this island of ancient culinary tradition where in a sense it all began, strikes me as a most encouraging portent for the continuing renaissance of Italian cooking.

MENU FOR A BARONIAL BANQUET

ANTIPASTI

CROCCHETTE DI CAPELLI D'ANGELO
Angel-hair pasta croquettes with cheese

FRITTELLE DI ZUCCA
Pumpkin fritters

COZZE RIPIENE
Baked stuffed mussels

I PRIMI

MACCHERONI COL CAVOLFIORE
Macaroni with cauliflower

SPAGHETTI CON SALSA DI LENTICCHIE
Spaghetti with lentil sauce

ANELLETTI ALLA SICILIANA
*Pasta rings baked with aubergines (eggplant)
and tomatoes*

I SECONDI

PASTICCIO DI FAGIANO
Pheasant pâté

MEDAGLIONI DI POLLO
Glazed medallions of chicken

SARDE ALLA REGALEALI
Sardines baked in orange

LE VERDURE

INSALATA DI FINOCCHI
Fennel salad

FUNGHI AL MARSALA
Mushrooms with Marsala

INSALATA DI LIMONI
Sliced lemon salad

I DOLCI

CASSATA DI PISTACCHIO
Pistachio ice cream gâteau

GELATINA DI MANDARINO
Tangerine gelatine

CANNOLI ALLA CANNELLA
Cinnamon cannoli

Although this is a menu for a banquet, each individual dish is so delicious that I have given the recipes to serve six in order that it might be enjoyed more frequently. One could construct three menus from the several choices for each course, or a light meal serving simply the sardines baked in orange and the fennel salad, for example. The delectable mushrooms with Marsala could even be a main course, preceded by an antipasto and/or followed by dessert.

Remember that the pasta course should always be served separately, never simultaneously with another course. In Italy, even for a buffet, the pasta is brought to the table after the antipasti and the plates changed for the next course. Please, no smörgasbords with Italian pasta!

Suggested Wines With the first three courses, nothing would be more appropriate than the Regaleali white, rosé and red, all exported to the United Kingdom and the United States. Until their new dessert wine comes on the market, a good alternative with the sweet would be the ambrosial Malvasia delle Lipari, made from grapes grown on the Aeolian Islands. It is a rich, fragrant wine, smooth and moderately sweet.

CROCCHETTE DI CAPELLI D'ANGELO
Angel-hair pasta croquettes with cheese

3½ oz/100 g piece of caciocavallo cheese (or Emmental)
10 oz/300 g angel-hair pasta
4 eggs
3½ oz/scant 1 cup/100 g grated Parmesan cheese
4 oz/1 cup/125 g fine dry breadcrumbs
oil for deep frying
salt and pepper

Cut the cheese into little cubes and set aside. Cook the pasta for 4 minutes in a large pan of boiling salted water. Drain, mix in 2 of the eggs, the Parmesan and salt and pepper.

Shape this pasta mixture into walnut-size balls and insert a cube of cheese in each one. Beat the remaining eggs. Dip each ball into the egg and coat with breadcrumbs. Deep-fry until golden in very hot oil. Drain on paper towels, arrange on a platter, and serve.

FRITTELLE DI ZUCCA
Pumpkin fritters

2 lb/1 kg pumpkin, whole or in pieces
3 eggs
1 tbsp chopped mint
2 cloves garlic, chopped
pinch of ground cinnamon
3½ oz/⅔ cup/100 g plain (all-purpose) flour
oil for deep frying
salt and pepper

Cook the pumpkin in the oven at 350°F/180°C/Mark 4 for 30 minutes. Discard the seeds and filaments, then scrape out the pulp with a fork.

Make a paste by mixing the pulp with 1 egg, the mint, garlic, cinnamon and salt and pepper. Shape into walnut-size balls. Beat the remaining 2 eggs. Roll the pumpkin balls in flour, dip in the egg and deep-fry in very hot oil until golden. Drain on paper towels, arrange on a platter and serve.

COZZE RIPIENE
Baked stuffed mussels

4½ lb/2 kg fresh mussels
2 oz/½ cup/50 g grated Parmesan cheese
3½ oz/½ cup/100 g cooked spinach, chopped
4 cloves garlic, chopped
grated peel of 1 lemon
1 egg
2 oz/½ cup/50 g fine dry breadcrumbs
4 tbsp extra virgin olive oil
salt and pepper

Discard any mussels that are open. Wash the mussels well and put in a large saucepan over medium heat until they open. Remove the meat and set the shells aside.

Mix together the remaining ingredients except breadcrumbs and oil, and season with salt and pepper. Place each mussel on a half shell and spread generously with the mixture. Sprinkle with breadcrumbs and drizzle over olive oil. Bake for 10 minutes in the oven at 400°F/200°C/Mark 6. Serve while still hot.

MACCHERONI COL CAVOLFIORE
Macaroni with cauliflower

1 medium cauliflower
1 lb/450 g macaroni
3¹/₂ oz/scant 1 cup/100 g fine dry breadcrumbs
4 fl oz/¹/₂ cup/100 ml extra virgin olive oil
6 anchovy fillets in oil
4 cloves garlic, chopped
3¹/₂ oz/³/₄ cup/100 g stoned (pitted) black olives
salt and pepper

Detach the florets from the base of the cauliflower. Cook the base in a large pan of salted boiling water for about 10 minutes, then remove and discard it and drop the macaroni and florets into the boiling water. Cook until *al dente*.

Stir-fry the breadcrumbs with 4 tablespoons of the olive oil. In another pan, sauté the anchovies and garlic in the remaining oil. Add the olives. Drain the pasta and florets. Stir in the olive sauce, season and sprinkle with breadcrumbs and serve.

SPAGHETTI CON SALSA DI LENTICCHIE
Spaghetti with lentil sauce

7 oz/1 cup/200 g brown lentils
3¹/₂ oz/100 g pancetta
1 onion
2 fl oz/¹/₄ cup/50 ml extra virgin olive oil
¹/₂ glass white wine
pinch of powdered saffron
1 bay leaf
1¹/₄ lb/600 g spaghetti
salt and pepper

Pasticcio di fagiano

Soak the lentils for at least 12 hours in cold water beforehand.

Stir-fry the pancetta with the onion in the oil over low heat until transparent. Add the lentils, a glass of water, the white wine, saffron and bay leaf. Cover and cook for 30 minutes over low heat. Purée through a food mill or food processor and reheat.

Cook the spaghetti until *al dente* in boiling salted water. Pour over the sauce and serve.

ANELLETTI ALLA SICILIANA
Pasta rings baked with aubergines (eggplant) and tomatoes

1 lb/450 g anelletti (or any small, ring-shaped pasta)
3 tbsp extra virgin olive oil
7 fl oz/scant 1 cup/200 ml tomato sauce
3 aubergines (eggplants)
oil for deep frying
3½ oz/100 g provolone cheese (or Emmental), thinly sliced
1 oz/2 tbsp/25 g butter
1 bunch basil leaves
3½ oz/100 g ricotta cheese, thinly sliced or crumbled
3 hard-boiled eggs
salt and pepper

Cook the pasta in boiling salted water, taking care to keep it very *al dente*. Drain and mix in the olive oil and the tomato sauce.

Thinly slice the aubergines and deep-fry in very hot oil. Drain on paper towels. Thinly slice the hard-boiled eggs. Grease a spring-clip (springform) pan with the butter and line it with alternating slices of aubergine and egg.

Mix the pasta with the remaining aubergines, the basil and the cheeses and fill the pan with the mixture. Cook in the oven at 400°F/200°C/Mark 6 for about 20 minutes. Unmold and serve.

PASTICCIO DI FAGIANO
Pheasant pâté

1 pheasant
3½ oz/100 g thinly sliced pork fat
3½ oz/7 tbsp/100 g butter
1 bay leaf
1 tbsp juniper berries
2 fl oz/¼ cup/50 ml Marsala
2 oz/½ cup/50 g soft fresh breadcrumbs
3½ oz/6 tbsp/100 g chopped ham
2 egg yolks
3½ oz/1 cup/100 g pistachio nuts
1 small black truffle, diced
salt and pepper
whipped cream (optional)

Clean the pheasant, cover with slices of pork fat and tie. Place in a casserole with 1 oz/2 tbsp/25 g of the butter, the bay leaf, juniper berries, and salt and pepper and cook in a preheated oven at 350°F/180°C/Mark 4 for about 1½ hours. Remove the pheasant from the casserole. Deglaze the cooking juices with the Marsala over medium heat. Discard the bay leaf and add the breadcrumbs.

Remove the pheasant meat from the bone and purée half of it through a food mill or food processor together with the ham and the cooking juices. Roughly chop the rest of the pheasant meat and add it to the purée with the egg yolks, pistachio nuts, the truffle and remaining butter. Mix well. Fill a mold compactly with the mixture and refrigerate for several hours.

Unmold by dipping the mold into warm water and decorate with whipped cream, if desired.

MEDAGLIONI DI POLLO
Glazed medallions of chicken

1 chicken
2 veal bones with marrow
1 carrot
1 bunch parsley
1 onion
1 celery stalk
1 bay leaf
1 pig's trotter (foot)
1 egg white
5 oz/150 g foie gras
1 black truffle
salt and pepper

In a large saucepan place the chicken, veal bones, vegetables, bay leaf and pig's trotter. Add salt and enough water to cover (about 40 fl oz/5 cups/1.1 liters). Bring to the boil, and cook over low heat for 1½ hours.

Drain the chicken, take the meat off the bone, and slice. Strain the broth through a colander and set aside to cool. Remove the surface fat. Clarify the broth by beating in the egg white, then bring to the boil and strain. Pour some of the broth into the bottom of 6 small molds and refrigerate until set.

Over the gelatine place a layer of dark meat just under ¼ in/0.5 cm thick. Over this, spread a little foie gras, and cover with a piece of white meat in such a way that the surface of the medallion is level. Place a slice of truffle in the center and cover with broth. Refrigerate for several hours until set. Unmold the medallions, arrange on a platter and serve.

SARDE ALLA REGALEALI
Sardines baked in orange

2¼ lb/1 kg fresh sardines

40 fl oz/5 cups/1 liter oil for deep frying

3 handfuls fresh breadcrumbs

3 oranges

3½ oz/½ cup/100 g raisins soaked in water

8 oz/1 cup/225 g pine nuts

6 tbsp extra virgin olive oil

salt and pepper

Cut open each sardine, discard the head and divide into 2 fillets. Arrange in a greased casserole; reserve. Deep-fry the breadcrumbs in very hot oil. Drain on paper towels and mix with the grated peel of 1 orange, the raisins and pine nuts.

Squeeze the juice from 1 orange and pour 3 tablespoons over the sardines. Pour over the olive oil, cover with the breadcrumbs, salt and pepper and bake in the oven at 350°F/180°C/Mark 4 for 20 minutes. Remove from the oven, decorate with slices of the remaining oranges and serve.

INSALATA DI FINOCCHI
Fennel salad

5 fennel bulbs

salt and pepper

1 tbsp lemon juice

4 tbsp extra virgin olive oil

Wash the fennel and discard the hard outer leaves. Cut each bulb lengthwise into quarters and slice thinly. Arrange on a serving dish and season with salt, pepper, the lemon juice and olive oil.

FUNGHI AL MARSALA
Mushrooms with Marsala

2¼ lb/1 kg fresh porcini (or button) mushrooms

Medaglioni di pollo

1 tbsp extra virgin olive oil

1 oz/2 tbsp/25 g butter

salt and pepper

5 fl oz/⅔ cup/150 ml fine quality Marsala

Clean the mushrooms by carefully wiping with a cloth (do not wash them). Slice, then stir-fry over medium heat in the olive oil and butter for just a couple of minutes. Season with salt and pepper and pour over the Marsala. Cook until the liquid evaporates. Arrange on a platter and serve.

INSALATA DI LIMONI
Sliced lemon salad

6 lemons (with non-chemically treated skins)

salt and pepper

4 tbsp extra virgin olive oil

1 tbsp chopped parsley

Finely slice the lemons with their skins on, removing any seeds. Arrange on a platter and season with salt, pepper and olive oil. Sprinkle over the parsley and serve.

Cassata di pistacchio
Sarde alla Regaleali

Gelatina di mandarino

CASSATA DI PISTACCHIO
Pistachio ice cream gâteau

1 lb/2 cups/450 g ricotta cheese
10 oz/2½ cups/300 g icing (confectioners') sugar
2 lb/1 kg watermelon, seeds discarded
3½ oz/⅓ cup/100 g pistachio nuts
10 oz/300 g almond paste
7 oz/1 cup/200 g candied fruit

Mix three-quarters of the ricotta with the sugar. Scoop the flesh from the watermelon, put the pulp through a food mill and mix with half the ricotta. Transfer the mixture to an ice cream maker and freeze.

Process the nuts until they are powdered, and mix with the almond paste. Line a mold with the paste and refrigerate for 2 hours. Fill the mold with the ricotta mixture, level with the back of a knife, then quickly unmold. Decorate the top with the remaining ricotta and the candied fruit and serve immediately.

GELATINA DI MANDARINO
Tangerine gelatine

8 oz/1 cup/225 g sugar
3 tbsp powdered gelatine
18 fl oz/2¼ cups/500 ml freshly squeezed tangerine juice
3 tbsp rum
6 oranges

Put the sugar in a saucepan, add a glass of water and boil for 2 minutes. Melt the gelatine in a little warm water and add the tangerine juice and rum. Strain and refrigerate in a bowl for several hours until the mixture has set.

Cut off the tops of the oranges to form baskets and carefully scoop out the insides. Break the gelatine mixture with a fork, fill the oranges and serve.

CANNOLI ALLA CANNELLA
Cinnamon cannoli

For the cannoli:
10 oz/2 cups/300 g plain (all-purpose) flour
8 oz/1 cup/225 g granulated sugar
1 tbsp cocoa powder
1 tsp ground cinnamon
2 oz/4 tbsp/50 g butter
2 fl oz/¼ cup/50 ml Marsala
1 egg, beaten
12 cannoli tubes (special metal pastry cylinders)
60 fl oz/7½ cups/1.7 liters oil for deep-frying
For the filling:
18 oz/2¼ cups/500 g ricotta cheese
2 oz/¼ cup/50 g candied orange peel, diced
2 oz/¼ cup/50 g candied citron peel, diced
2 oz/¼ cup/50 g candied cherries
2 oz/½ cup/50 g icing (confectioners') sugar
2 oz/⅓ cup/50 g bitter chocolate, coarsely grated

Make a dough mixing the flour, 2 oz/¼ cup/50 g of the granulated sugar, the cocoa powder, a pinch of cinnamon, the butter and Marsala (as explained on page 00). Knead until smooth and roll into a thin sheet. Cut into 4-5 in/10-12.5 cm rounds, and wrap each one around a cannoli tube. Seal the sides where they join by brushing with egg, and deep-fry in very hot oil. Drain on paper towels. When cool, carefully slide out the tubes.

Rub the ricotta with the rest of the cinnamon and granulated sugar through a sieve. Add the candied orange and citron peel and fill the cannoli using a piping (pastry) bag. Decorate with a cherry at each end. Dust with the icing sugar and chocolate and serve.

BASIC TECHNIQUES

HOMEMADE PASTA

In Italy, fresh pasta is made at home with plain (all-purpose) flour and eggs. Water and oil are never added. Semolina flour is used only in commercial dry pasta.

Because flour reacts in different ways depending not only on its quality but on the climate where it is being used, it would be misleading to give exact measurements for pasta dough recipes. I have given the amounts that work for me in my kitchen in Chianti, using the type of flour we have in Toscana. You will have to adjust these to your particular situation.

In general, 1 large egg shoud be used for every 3¼ oz/⅔ cup/100 g flour. Because the specific weight of ingredients varies (e.g. the specific weight of half a cup of flour is about half that of the same amount of sugar), it is better to calculate by weight rather than by cups.

Making fresh pasta is not as complicated as it may sound. It does require a certain skill and that will come easily with practice. Here I have tried to describe the process in a simple, accessible and workable way.

Heap the flour onto the work surface. Make a well in the center and break the eggs into it. With a fork, begin to mix the eggs with the flour, little by little absorbing the surrounding flour.

When the eggs have been absorbed, begin to work the mixture with your fingertips until it forms a paste. Then knead with the heel of your hands, working in this way for about 10 minutes until the dough has formed a ball that is smooth, elastic and not too hard.

Sprinkle a light veil of flour over the work surface and flatten the ball of dough with a rolling pin, beginning from the center and rolling out into the shape of a circle. Repeat the rolling-out operation until the sheet of dough is paper-thin. During this operation it is important to keep the work surface floured in order that the pasta does not stick. To do this, lift the dough off the work surface by rolling it around the pin, so that you can lightly dust the surface beneath with flour.

When the pasta sheet has been rolled out to the desired thinness, cut it into the shape required by the recipe, i.e. tagliatelle, ravioli, etc.

SHORT PASTRY (PIECRUST DOUGH) (pasta frolla)

This pastry dough is used for sweet tarts and little pastries as well as for some savory pies. It is based on a ratio of flour to butter, egg yolks and the same amount of sugar when the crust is sweet, or some salt when savoury. Water is never added because it would cause the dough to lose its crumbly consistency, which is what the word *frolla* means.

In general, for 7 oz/1½ cups/200 g of plain (all-purpose) flour, 3½ oz/½ cup/100 g of granulated sugar, the same amount of butter and 1 egg yolk is required. As I said with regard to making pasta dough, depending on the quality of flour, the climate and other particulars of a recipe, the amounts of these ingredients can vary. This is not a difficult dough to make.

Heap the flour onto the work surface. Make a well in the center and put into it the butter, broken into pieces, softened but not melted, the sugar and egg yolks. Work with your fingertips until the mixture resembles coarse oatmeal. Knead briefly until the dough comes together. Wrap the dough in plastic wrap and refrigerate for 1 hour. Allow to return to room temperature before rolling out.

Put dough between 2 large sheets of plastic wrap and flatten it out, first with the heel of the hand, and then with a rolling pin, to the required thickness. Remove the top sheet of wrap. Place your chosen flan or tart pan upside-down on top of the sheet of dough. Reverse quickly with the help of a large spatula. Remove the remaining sheet of wrap and press the dough lightly with your fingers in order to line the pan smoothly. Trim the edge with a knife and bake according to the recipe.

PUFF PASTRY (pasta sfoglia)

This pastry dough, as its name implies, puffs up when it is baked. It is light and flaky, and because it is composed of equal weights of flour and butter, it is also very rich. Water is added but not sugar. Again, it would be misleading to give measurements for the amount of water necessary. With practice, your hands will develop a sensitivity in this regard. In general, for 8 oz/1⅔ cups/225 g plain (all-purpose) flour and the same weight of butter you will need to add half that amount of water. Making this pastry requires a good amount of time, but the only difficulty in the process is that the butter block must be of the same consistency as the dough. If it is too hard it will tear the dough when you roll it out.

For the dough: Reserve one-fifth of the flour for the butter block and heap the rest on the work surface. Make a well in the center and put into it a pinch of salt and 3½ fl oz/½ cup/110 ml water. Work with your fingers until the mixture resembles coarse oatmeal. Knead the dough, adding water a little at a time as needed, until it is homogenous and very elastic. Form the dough into a ball, wrap in plastic wrap and refrigerate for 30 minutes.

For the butter block: Soften the butter, and then blend it with your fingers, with the remaining one-fifth of flour until it has the same consistency as the dough. Place a piece of plastic wrap on the work surface. Place the dough on top, and with a rolling pin flatten the dough into a square about ½ in/1 cm thick. Place the butter block in the center and fold the corners of the dough toward the center, over the butter block, completely enclosing it like an envelope, without overlapping the dough. Press down gently with the fingers in order to seal. Wrap in plastic wrap and refrigerate again for 20 minutes.

To finish: Unwrap the dough and place it on a sheet of plastic wrap. Roll out the dough into a rectangle about ¼ in/0.5 cm thick. Fold the rectangle into thirds and flatten lightly with the rolling pin. Wrap the dough in plastic wrap and refrigerate again for 20 minutes. This concludes the first *giro* or turn. You must repeat this step 5 more times for a total of 6 turns. At the sixth one, after folding the rectangle into thirds, roll out the puff pastry dough to the required size and oven bake.

MAKING MEAT BROTH

Italian broth is not the same as French stock. The Italian way of making broth is to use relatively lean cuts of meat without the bone and some vegetables. It is flavorful, light and easy on the digestion. When you are making gelatine for pâté, etc., some bones as well as a pig's trotter (foot) are added.

A good recipe for making beef broth is to put in a saucepan 1lb/450 g beef, 1 lb/450 g veal, 1 celery stalk, 1 peeled carrot, 1 small onion, 1 bay leaf, 1 bunch Italian parsley. Add 105 fl oz/13 cups/3 liters water and bring to a boil. Turn the heat to low and cook for about 3 hours. At the end there will be about 40 fl oz/5 cups/1.1 liters of broth. Do not skim the broth while it is cooking, because that reduces much of its nutritive value, just allow it to be absorbed into the broth. Add salt only when the cooking is finished. Pass the broth through a fine sieve, leave to cool completely and refrigerate. Take off the fat that solidifies on the surface, and clarify the broth by reboiling for a couple of minutes, adding some chopped

white meat or the white of an egg. Strain again.

Chicken broth is made in the same way, using a whole, cleaned chicken. Broth made from a mixture of beef, veal and chicken is also excellent. Remember that it must always be refrigerated, and if you do not use it within 12 hours it must be frozen.

BOILING MEAT

The best meats for boiling are chicken, capon and cuts of beef and veal with some fat content such as rump roast, skirt (flank) and brisket.

In a large saucepan put enough water to cover the meat. Bring to the boil, add salt and put in the meat. When it returns to a boil, cover and simmer for the time specified in the recipe. When the quantities are to serve 6, 3 hours will be required for beef, 2 hours for veal, 1½ hours for capon, and 1 hour for chicken. The larger the quantity of meat, the longer it must be cooked in order to bring out its full flavor.

At the end of cooking, remove the meat and pass the broth through a fine sieve. Remember to always refrigerate the broth and to freeze it if not used within 12 hours.

ROASTING MEAT

The classic Italian way of roasting chicken, duck, pigeon (squab), pheasant, veal, lamb and all white meat is to cook them slowly for a very long time in the oven or on top of the stove. Cooked in this way the fat has time to dissolve and can be drawn off at the end, the meat is very tender and easily detached from the bone and not at all dry.

To roast in this way you will need a heavy aluminum casserole in which the cooking juices can build up. Enameled ware and stainless steel do not have the same effect. Always keep the casserole uncovered and only toward the end of cooking should you add a little liquid, broth or wine. To deglaze, remove the meat and draw off the fat. Scrape up the cooking residue from the bottom of the

casserole with a wooden spoon, add a little liquid, heat for a few minutes until it dissolves, strain, reheat and pour over the roast.

BRAISING MEAT

For braising, use succulent cuts of meat with some fat content, such as leg, rump roast, topside and silverside (round), shank and chuck and blade (shoulder). Cook in a heavy aluminum casserole over high heat with butter, oil or whatever cooking fat the recipe requires, and vegetables.

Brown the meat on all sides in the cooking fat, add the chopped vegetables and one glass of liquid broth or wine. Cover, turn the heat to low and simmer. Keep moist by adding more liquid a little at a time. Never add more liquid until the previous amount has been absorbed. Braised meat can be cooked on top of the stove or in the oven. Cooked in the oven the meat will absorb less liquid.

When the meat has finished cooking, pass the vegetables through a food mill. If the resulting sauce is too liquid, reduce it by cooking for a few minutes. If it is too thick, add more liquid, reheat and stir frequently to keep it from sticking to the pan. The sauce obtained from braising meat in this way is excellent, dark brown and full of flavor. Remember that you must use heavy aluminum, not enameled ware or stainless steel.

DEEP-FRYING

Deep-fry in quality extra virgin olive oil and the results will be light, fragrant, crisp and even healthy, because extra virgin olive oil can be heated at a higher temperature than any other kind of oil without releasing toxins.

The oil should be heated to a temperature of 380°F/190°C. It can be measured without a thermometer, by dropping a tiny piece of bread into the oil. When it blisters around the edges, the oil is ready, which is before it reaches the smoking point. Use enough oil so that the food can float freely. Once oil has been used for frying, it must be discarded.

ACKNOWLEDGEMENTS

I wish to thank the following people for their
kind collaboration, and in particular John Meis for his assistance
throughout the project:

LELE GANI AND NICOLETTA DI SAMBUY · *Castello di Monale*

GIOVANNA CAMELI · *Genova*

LIDIA ORSI · *Ca'Mera*

CARLOTTA MARCELLO · *Levada*

GRAZIA GAZZONI · *Bologna*

NANNI GUISO · *Sardegna*

PIERO AND GIULIANA DORAZIO · *Todi*

BEVERLEY AND BILL PEPPER · *Todi*

STEFANINA ALDOBRANDINI · *Roma*

FRANCO SANTASILIA · *Napoli*

MARCHESA LEOPOLDINA CARACCIOLO · *Napoli*

GLORIA REALE · *Lecce*

GIUSEPPE AND FRANCA TASCA D'ALMERITA · *Palermo*

Thanks also to the wonderful cooks, especially to
my invaluable Romola at Badia, and Anna Forcellini who
taught me the great art of cooking:

MARIA · *Genova*

BERNARDINA · *Sardegna*

ANNETTA · *Umbria*

GERARDO MODUGNO · *Napoli*

MARIO LO MENZO · *Palermo*

INDEX TO THE RECIPES